The
Healthy Everyday
KITCHEN

The
Healthy Everyday
KITCHEN

*Feel-good food for
happy and healthy eating*

This edition published by Parragon Books Ltd in 2017 and distributed by

Parragon Inc.
440 Park Avenue South, 13th Floor
New York, NY 10016
www.parragon.com/love-food

LOVE FOOD is an imprint of Parragon Books Ltd

ISBN 978-1-4748-8107-4

Printed in China

Main introduction by Robin Donovan
Cover photography by Tony Briscoe

—————————— Notes for the Reader ——————————

This book uses standard kitchen measuring spoons and cups. All spoon and cup measurements are level unless otherwise indicated. Unless otherwise stated, milk is assumed to be whole, eggs are large, individual fruits and vegetables are medium, pepper is freshly ground black pepper, and salt is table salt. A pinch of salt is calculated as $1/16$ of a teaspoon. Unless otherwise stated, all root vegetables should be peeled prior to using.

The times given are only an approximate guide. Preparation times differ according to the techniques used by different people, and the cooking times may also vary from those given.

Please note that any ingredients stated as being optional are not included in the nutritional values provided. The nutritional values given are approximate and provided only as a guideline, they do not account for individual cooks, measuring scales, and portion sizes. The nutritional values provided are per serving or per item.

For best results, use a food thermometer when cooking meat. Check the latest government guidelines for current advice.

For gluten-free recipes, the publisher has been careful to select recipes that contain gluten-free products. Any prepared ingredients that could potentially contain gluten have been listed as "gluten free," so readers know to check they are gluten free. However, always read labels carefully and, if necessary, check with the manufacturer. For vegan recipes, the publisher has been careful to select recipes that do not contain animal products. Any prepared ingredients that could potentially contain animal products have been listed as "vegan," so readers know to look for the vegan version. However, always read labels carefully and, if necessary, check with the manufacturer.

CONTENTS

THE HEALTHY EVERYDAY KITCHEN

Nowadays, it seems everyone is talking about a new way to eat "healthy," but what exactly does this mean? For starters, many minor everyday health problems and serious illnesses can be prevented, improved, or even eliminated by choosing the right diet. And there's plenty of science to back up the idea that what you eat can have an effect on your energy, vitality, mood, brain function, and even your appearance. However, with so many lifestyle options to choose from, how do you decide what's best for you and your family?

The Healthy Everyday Kitchen is designed to bring numerous diet plans together in one book: superfoods, clean eating, low sugar, protein, gluten-free, vegan, and cleansing. It's the go-to guide for all the latest health trends. Combining several dietary plans in one ultimate, health-eating cookbook, it's a handy resource that you can use to explore different ways of cooking and eating to find the plan—or combination of plans—that works best for you.

In addition to the details of several different eating plans, you'll find recipes that are made with healthy ingredients—and that are easy to fit into a busy life. Each chapter includes a range of family-friendly recipes, from breakfast to dessert, that adhere to that lifestyle. You can pick and choose recipes from different chapters, either to explore different ways of eating or simply to find the foods that you and your family like best.

Nutritional information for every recipe helps you keep track of what you're eating, and you can be assured that every dish offers benefits to your health and well-being.

SUPERFOODS

If you're feeling run down and in need of a boost, go to the Superfoods chapter. Superfoods are nutrient-dense ingredients that deliver antioxidants, phytochemicals, essential vitamins, minerals, protein, complex carbohydrates, and "good" fats, nutrients that are crucial for growth, repair, immunity, essential metabolic processes, reducing health risks, and boosting energy. You'll find ingredients here such as fruit and vegetables, nuts and seeds, and whole grains.

CLEAN EATING

If you're interested in cutting out refined, processed, and artificial ingredients, the Clean Eating chapter is a great resource. Clean eating means eating foods in their most natural, whole state, thereby maximizing their nutritional benefits. The Clean Eating plan provides recipes that are free of unwanted ingredients, such as refined grains and sugars, artificial flavors, colors, thickeners, preservatives, and other questionable additives. Instead, these dishes contain lean meats, fish, vegetables, fruits, nuts, and seeds. You'll discover that you can still enjoy your favorite foods, only they will be made with healthier (and fewer) ingredients. They'll taste better and be better for you.

PROTEIN

Protein is essential for rebuilding cells and is important to include in any diet, but it doesn't necessarily have to come from meat. The Protein chapter provides a range of recipes—both vegetarian and meat—that contain natural and healthy sources of protein. Ingredients such as legumes (beans), nuts and seeds, and eggs provide plenty of healthy protein.

LOW SUGAR

Too much sugar has an impact on your health and well-being and is a risk factor for type-two diabetes, obesity, sleep disturbances, decreased energy, and mood disorders. If your goal is to cut down your family's sugar intake, the Low Sugar chapter provides the lowdown on sugar and how to eliminate added sugars from your diet.

GLUTEN FREE

The Gluten-Free trend has spread like wildfire, and it seems as though everyone has gone gluten-free, but why? This chapter explains all about gluten intolerance (as well as the much rarer celiac disease) and provides recipes for delicious gluten-free dishes.

VEGAN

If you're used to eating meat and dairy products regularly, a vegan diet may sound extreme, but with the Vegan chapter, you don't have to do a major lifestyle overhaul. You can experiment with vegan cooking for one meal, or commit to a day or week of vegan eating.

CLEANSING

When you feel you've overdone it—say, after a vacation or celebration—and you need to get back on track, take a look at the Cleansing chapter. It details a plan for nourishing your body with all the plant chemicals, vitamins, minerals, and fiber it needs to run at optimum efficiency. The recipes in this chapter are bursting with healthy fruits, vegetables, whole grains, nuts and seeds, legumes, oily fish, and other ingredients that are known to boost your immune system, increase "friendly" bacteria in the digestive tract, and assist the liver, the body's main detoxifying organ.

HEALTHY MENU PLANNING

Each chapter provides a comprehensive introduction to all the information you need to try out the lifestyle for a week, a day, or even just one meal. You'll gain real insight into what you need to know if you decide to follow one or more of these lifestyles indefinitely—or need to cook for someone who is doing so. You may discover just the right diet, or you may find that you enjoy mixing things up from meal to meal.

You may find slightly differing advice from chapter to chapter, but don't worry. These recipes are all designed to be enjoyed as part of a natural and wholesome diet, so unless you want specifically to follow one particular lifestyle, you can use this book to draw up a menu that combines the best of all approaches.

So whether you're looking for delicous breakfast inspiration, sustaining lunch ideas, superb snacks, mighty main meals, or delicious desserts, this book has it covered.

SUPERFOODS

WHAT IS A SUPERFOOD?

"Superfoods" have been celebrated by nutritionists as being beneficial for health and well-being for years. These nutrient-dense ingredients offer a bundle of essential vitamins, minerals, protein, complex carbohydrates, and good monounsaturated and polyunsaturated fats. A balanced intake of these nutrients is crucial for energy, growth, repair, immunity, and essential metabolic processes. However, the good news doesn't stop there—superfoods are also rich in antioxidants and phytochemicals, which can help protect us against cancers, coronary heart disease, strokes, diabetes, and obesity. No wonder we so often hear that superfoods should be right at the top of our shopping list.

Superfoods can be bought easily from supermarkets and health–food stores and are often inexpensive. Thanks to their health–boosting qualities, they can almost be called "natural medicines," but no prescription is required, and there are no negative side effects as long as they are eaten as part of a balanced diet.

The brighter the color of a fruit or vegetable, the more beneficial to health it will probably be. Choose from deep purple blueberries, ruby red strawberries and raspberries, bright orange squashes, carrots, and mangoes, and deep green broccoli and kale. Plant foods are packed with antioxidants and phytochemicals (biologically active plant chemicals). These help to reduce the activity of free radicals—harmful compounds produced by the body that damage DNA and body tissues—and so they are believed to help protect the body against cancer.

Wash or scrub fruits and vegetables and eat them with the skins on when possible to boost their fiber, vitamin, and mineral levels. There's no need to peel apples, pears, peaches, or young carrots. This is an easy way to add natural soluble fiber to your diet, which will help stave off midmorning or midafternoon munchies, lower cholesterol, and protect against bowel cancer.

Plants aren't the only superfoods. Nuts, seeds, whole grains, oily fish, and plain yogurt with live cultures are other examples of nutrient–dense, power–packed ingredients.

There's a lot of truth in the expression "we are what we eat," and eating a range of superfoods should help you to feel fitter, lighter, and more energized, and to cope with the hustle and bustle of modern living, while improving your long–term health.

20 FABULOUS SUPERFOODS

1. GO FOR GREEN

The deeper green vegetables are, the more lutein and zeaxanthin (two antioxidants related to vitamin A) they will probably contain. Broccoli, cabbage, Swiss chard, kale, arugula, spinach, and watercress are rich in chlorophyll, which assists with the oxygenation and health of blood cells, so helping to fight fatigue. They are also good sources of the B vitamins, especially folic acid, as well as immune-boosting vitamin C and vitamin K for strong bones and healthy blood clotting. Kale is a useful source of iron. Broccoli and cauliflower belong to the cabbage family and are good sources of sulfurous compounds that may help protect against cancer.

2. RED FRUIT BONANZA

Summery red berries, such as strawberries and raspberries, are rich in vitamin C, which aids healing and fights infection, and fiber. Cranberries help block bacterial growth, especially in the urinary tract. Their relative, the blueberry, is high in antioxidants, pectin to help lower cholesterol, and vitamin C. Pomegranates also contain antioxidant vitamins, as well as iron and fiber. Although high in water, red-fleshed watermelons contain antioxidants, folic acid, potassium, and vitamins A and C. Pink and ruby grapefruits, along

with other members of the citrus family and kiwis, are bursting with vitamin C, as well as minerals and antioxidants. Power-packed with antioxidants, iron, fiber, and vitamin C, dried goji berries make a great pantry standby. Tomatoes get their red color from lycopene, a carotenoid pigment that, along with the other antioxidants tomatoes contain, may help protect against free-radical damage and prostate cancer and prevent blood clots.

3. RED VEG BONANZA

Red beets get their red pigment from the antioxidants betalains, which help protect against free-radical damage and may help reduce the risk of heart disease, and they provide a wide range of vitamins, minerals, and carbohydrates. All bell peppers contain vitamin C, but red bell peppers contain the most, followed by orange and yellow, then green. They are rich in antioxidants and bioflavonoids, which help neutralize free-radical damage and, therefore, are thought to help protect against cancer.

4. SUNSHINE FRUITS AND VEGETABLES

Rich in beta-carotene, this bright orange group contains carrots, butternut squash and other squashes, sweet potatoes, papayas, mangoes, and apricots. Beta-carotene is needed by the body to make vitamin A, an antioxidant thought to help protect against cancer, and that is important for the integrity of each cell and to boost the immune system.

5. FALL'S APPLES AND PEARS

Apples are rich in pectin (the setting agent in preserves), which helps to remove excess cholesterol and toxic metals from the digestive tract while stimulating the growth of friendly bacteria in the large intestine, boosting vitamin C, and providing a naturally sweet energy lift. Pears are healthy, too, and they are packed with fiber.

6. EGGS AND LOW-FAT AND PROBIOTIC YOGURTS

Eggs are power-packed with protein. Low-fat yogurts make a good replacement for cream as a dessert topping or base for frozen desserts, salad dressings, and marinades, and the calcium and phosphorus they contain helps boost bone strength. Yogurts with live cultures are thought to help maintain and promote healthy bacterial balance in the intestines and bowel, and strengthen your natural defenses, which is especially useful after a course of antibiotics, because these can kill good bacteria as well as bad,

7. FABULOUS FISH

Salmon, trout, mackerel, fresh tuna, and sardines are oily fish that are rich in protein, needed for growth and the maintenance of cells. They're packed with Omega-3 essential fatty acids, which help protect against heart and circulation problems and aid healthy development of the eyes and brain of a baby during pregnancy. They're a good source of minerals: selenium for growth and fertility, iodine for healthy function of the thyroid gland, vitamin B$_{12}$ for the nervous system, and vitamin D for healthy bones and teeth.

8. SUSTAINING WHOLE GRAINS

Avoid highly refined rice and flours. Choose brown rice for higher vitamin B levels and fiber. Opt for whole-wheat or multigrain flour for maximum fiber, or try wheat-free, gluten-free flours, such as buckwheat flour, brown rice flour, or hemp flour. Rolled oats and oatmeal make a sustaining, warming breakfast or muesli base, and taste great in cakes and baked goods. Cook oat or barley groats or wheat berries in boiling water as an alternative to rice. Look for whole-grain couscous and quinoa, the only grain to contain all the essential amino acids the body requires. Rich in fiber, whole grains leave you feeling fuller for longer and help maintain a healthy digestive system, lower cholesterol, and aid good heart health.

9. POWER LEGUMES

Choose legumes either dried or canned in water for a cheap, low-fat base to any meal. They taste great mixed with vegetables and spices, and a little added to meat or poultry makes a meal go farther. Dried legumes include cannellini beans, great northern beans, and red kidney beans, to name just a few. They all require soaking in cold water overnight and then boiling in water before use. Red lentils, which make a good base for dal; brown lentils, which are great as a salad base; or the larger green lentils, can all be used without soaking and are a good source of protein, the B vitamins, and minerals. The fiber they contain helps to lower blood cholesterol, while the starch is digested and absorbed by the body slowly to give a sustained energy release.

10. NUTS AND SEEDS

Packed with protein, nuts supply many of the same minerals that meat does, such as the B vitamins, phosphorus, iron, copper, and potassium, so are good for vegetarians. They are high in fat, so add them to dishes in small amounts. Nuts are one of the richest sources of vitamin E, but it is destroyed when they are roasted, so eat them raw when you can. Supermarkets now sell hemp, flaxseed, and chia seeds as well as pumpkin, sunflower, and sesame seeds. Ideally, grind or chop them, so the body is able to absorb as many of the nutrients as possible. Finely ground seeds can be used in much the same way as ground almonds (almond meal). Like nuts, seeds are high in calories. Flaxseed are rich in the B vitamins, magnesium, and manganese, plus Omega-3 and -6 essential fatty acids. Chia seeds are also a good source of essential fatty acids as well as calcium, iron, copper, and zinc. Hemp seeds are the only seeds to contain all the essential amino acids.

11. DATES

A natural source of sweetness, dates contain fiber, potassium, manganese, magnesium, and vitamins A, B$_6$, and K. Due to the fiber content, they're thought to help maintain a healthy colon.

12. SECRETS OF SOY

The Chinese and Japanese have long enjoyed soybeans and tofu. Soy is rich in protein and contains all the essential amino acids, vitamin E and the B vitamins, calcium, iron, and antioxidants, while being low in fat. Fiber-rich baby green soybeans (edamame) are sold frozen. Soy milk, made from the soaked ground beans, can be used instead of dairy milk in most recipes. Tofu is made from soybeans; dice it and add to vegetable stews, noodle dishes or soups, or marinade it in soy sauce, ginger, and garlic and then sauté, dice, and add to salads or stir-fries. Soy helps to protect against heart disease, osteoporosis, and menopausal symptoms.

13. AMAZING ALLIUMS

Garlic has been used for centuries to help fight infections, because it acts as an antimicrobial agent. Leeks are another allium (from the onion family) with superfood properties, and are particularly notable for their concentration of the B vitamin folate, while their antioxidant and flavonoid properties mean they help protect our blood vessels and blood cells.

14. JERUSALEM ARTICHOKES

Packed with inulin, these knobbly roots are thought to aid beneficial bacteria in the digestive tract, while their high fiber and water content help keep our bowels healthy. They are also a good source of potassium.

15. ENERGIZING BANANAS

A banana is a terrific high-energy snack, and a great source of natural fruit sugars, starch, and potassium to help regulate blood pressure and lower the risk of heart attacks and strokes. It is the only fruit to contain both the amino acid tryptophan and vitamin B_6, which together produce the natural chemical serotonin, making it a good-mood food.

16. AMAZING AVOCADOS

The avocado contains even more potassium than the banana. Thought to be one of the most nutritionally complete fruits, it is rich in vitamins, minerals, phytonutrients, the antioxidant lutein, and protein.

17. SEED SPROUTS

Think of seed sprouts, sometimes called sprouting seeds, as a nutritional powerhouse. As the seeds germinate and begin to sprout, their natural nutrients multiply to meet the growing needs of the young shoots. This makes them a good way to add a range of antioxidants and immune-boosting vitamins, minerals, and protein to a dish. As the seeds sprout, so the plant enzymes increase, and this aids digestion. Children younger than five, older adults, pregnant women, and those with a weakened immune system are particularly vulnerable to the bacteria that may be present on sprouts and so should not eat raw sprouts. Buy packaged sprouts from the supermarkets or grow them from a kit following the manufacturer's instructions and wash them well.

18. TURKEY

High in concentrated protein, skinless and boneless turkey is low in fat, saturated fat, and sodium.

19. DARK CHOCOLATE

Choose chocolate that has over 65 percent cocoa. The higher the cocoa content, the higher the flavonoids, which help to reduce infection and protect cells from damage. Dark chocolate also contains the mineral magnesium, which is needed for nerve and muscle function, and the amino acid tryptophan, which is used by the body to make serotonin.

20. GREEN TEA

Long favored by the Chinese, green tea contains an enhanced level of antioxidants. It is thought to have antibacterial and antiviral properties. Many people believe it can help boost metabolism, aid blood pressure, and reduce bad cholesterol.

RED BEET HASH

A vegetable hash is the perfect weekend brunch. This dish contains antioxidant-rich sweet potatoes, low-carbohydrate Jerusalem artichokes, and cholesterol-lowering beets.

SERVES: 4
PREP: 20 MINS   COOK: 40 MINS

12 ounces Jerusalem artichokes,
unpeeled and scrubbed
5½ raw beets (about 1 pound), cut into cubes
5 sweet potatoes (about 1½ pounds), cut into cubes
2 tablespoons olive oil
1 red onion, coarsely chopped
2 teaspoons mild paprika
½ teaspoon dry mustard
1 tablespoon fresh thyme leaves,
plus extra to garnish
4 eggs
salt and pepper (optional)

1. Halve any larger artichokes. Fill the bottom of a steamer halfway with water, bring to a boil, then add the artichokes to the water. Put the beets in one half of the steamer top, cover with a lid, and steam for 10 minutes. Put the sweet potatoes in the other half of the top so the color of the beets doesn't bleed into them. Cover with a lid again and steam for an additional 10 minutes, or until all the vegetables are just tender. Drain the artichokes, peel them, and cut them into cubes.

2. Heat 1 tablespoon of oil in a large skillet over medium heat. Add the red onion and sauté for 3–4 minutes, or until beginning to soften. Add the artichokes, beets, and sweet potatoes and cook for 10 minutes, or until browned.

3. Stir in the paprika, dry mustard, and thyme and season well with salt and pepper, if using. Make four spaces in the skillet, drizzle in the remaining oil, then crack an egg into each hole. Sprinkle the eggs with salt and pepper, if using. Cover and cook for 4–5 minutes, or until the eggs are cooked to your liking. Spoon onto plates and serve immediately, garnished with extra thyme.

DETOX WITH ARTICHOKES
Knobbly-looking Jerusalem artichokes contain several phytonutrients, which are thought to help detoxify the liver and boost gallbladder function. They are also considered to help digestion. What's more, they're packed with fiber, helping you to feel fuller for longer.

PER SERVING: 430 CALS | 12.6G FAT | 2.7G SAT FAT | 67.4G CARBS | 25.3G SUGARS | 11.1G FIBER | 14G PROTEIN | 560MG SODIUM

BANANA, GOJI, AND HAZELNUT BREAD

On mornings when you don't have time to eat breakfast before you leave for work, wrap a slice of this superfood-packed bread in parchment paper and eat when you get there.

MAKES: 10 SLICES
PREP: 20 MINS, PLUS COOLING   COOK: 1 HOUR

6 tablespoons butter, softened, plus extra to grease
½ cup firmly packed light brown sugar
2 eggs
3 bananas (about 1 pound), peeled and mashed
1 cup whole-wheat flour
1 cup all-purpose flour
2 teaspoons baking powder
½ cup coarsely chopped unblanched hazelnuts
⅓ cup goji berries
⅔ cup dried banana chips

1. Preheat the oven to 350°F. Grease a 9 x 5 x 3-inch loaf pan and line the bottom and two long sides with a piece of parchment paper.

2. Cream the butter and sugar together in a large bowl. Beat in the eggs, one at a time, then the bananas.

3. Put the flours and baking powder into a bowl and mix well. Add to the banana mixture and beat until smooth. Add the hazelnuts and goji berries and stir well.

4. Spoon the batter into the prepared pan, smooth the top flat, then sprinkle with the banana chips. Bake for 50–60 minutes, or until the loaf is well risen, has cracked slightly, and a toothpick inserted into the center comes out clean.

5. Let cool for 5 minutes, then loosen the edges with a blunt knife and turn out onto a wire rack. Let cool completely, then peel away the paper. Store in an airtight container for up to three days.

HIGH-ENERGY BANANAS
Naturally rich in fruit sugar and starch, bananas are a great energy-boosting food. They contain plenty of potassium, which can help to regulate blood pressure and lower the risk of heart attacks and strokes. They also contain the amino acid tryptophan and vitamin B6, which together help in the production of mood-boosting serotonin.

PER SLICE: 276 CALS | 10G FAT | 2.5G SAT FAT | 43G CARBS | 19G SUGARS | 3.5G FIBER | 5.5G PROTEIN | 320G SODIUM

FRUITY GRANOLA CUPS

Granola is easy to make, and a wonderful standby ingredient—
just add yogurt and fruit when you're ready for breakfast.

SERVES: 6
PREP: 25 MINS   COOK: 35 MINS

¼ cup steel-cut oats
1 cup rolled oats
½ cup coarsely chopped unblanched almonds
2 tablespoons pumpkin seeds
2 tablespoons sunflower seeds
2 tablespoons flaxseed, coarsely ground
½ teaspoon ground cinnamon
3 tablespoons maple syrup
1 tablespoon olive oil
¼ cup dried goji berries

TO SERVE (SERVES 2)

1 cup granola
juice of 1 orange
½ cup Greek-style plain yogurt
1 crisp, sweet apple, cored and coarsely grated
⅔ cup hulled and sliced strawberries
⅓ cup blueberries

1. Preheat the oven to 325°F. Put the steel-cut oats, rolled oats, and almonds in a bowl. Stir in the pumpkin seeds, sunflower seeds, and flaxseed, then the cinnamon, maple syrup, and oil.

2. Transfer the granola to a roasting pan, then spread into an even layer. Bake for 30–35 minutes, or until golden brown all over, stirring every 5–10 minutes and mixing any browner granola from the edges of the pan into the center after 15 minutes.

3. Stir in the goji berries, then let cool. Pack into an airtight container and store in the refrigerator for up to five days.

4. When ready to serve, spoon a scant ½ cup granola into each of two glasses or bowls, keeping a little back for the top. Moisten with the orange juice. Mix the yogurt with the apple and spoon it over the granola, then top with the strawberries and blueberries and sprinkle with the remaining granola.

PROTECTIVE FLAXSEED

Grinding flaxseed in a food processor, blender, or spice mill means you can use them in cooking in the same way as ground almonds (almond meal). It also means they are in a form that the body can process more easily, so that larger amounts of the essential omega-3 fatty acids, needed for heart health can be absorbed. They are rich in lignans, antioxidants that help protect the body against cancer, and in the B vitamins, minerals, and fiber.

PER SERVING: 402 CALS | 13.4G FAT | 1.6G SAT FAT | 57.6G CARBS | 28.7G SUGARS | 9.3G FIBER | 15G PROTEIN | TRACE SODIUM

AVOCADO AND FRUIT JUICE

Protect your body from the inside out with this fresh, fruity drink that is bursting with antioxidants.

SERVES: 1
PREP: 10 MINS

½ avocado, pitted, peeled, and coarsely chopped
¾ cup blueberries
¾ cup hulled strawberries
juice of 1 tangerine or small orange
½ cup cold water
small handful of crushed ice (optional)

1. Put the avocado, blueberries, strawberries, tangerine juice, and water into a food processor or blender and process until blended.

2. Add the crushed ice, if using, and process again until smooth. Pour into a glass and serve.

GOOD-FOR-YOU AVOCADO

Avocados may inhibit the growth of prostate cancer and, being high in oleic acid, they may also help to prevent breast cancer. They contain more of the carotenoid lutein than any other commonly consumed fruit. Lutein protects against macular degeneration and cataracts, two disabling age-related eye diseases. Eating avocados may also lower your cholesterol levels and, as an excellent source of glutathione, they even contain antiaging properties.

PER SERVING: 250 CALS | 15G FAT | 3.5G SAT FAT | 18G CARBS | 18G SUGARS | 6G FIBER | 3G PROTEIN | TRACE SODIUM

SHRIMP-FILLED BAKED SWEET POTATOES

We all love baked potatoes, and this healthy lunch is topped with low-fat cottage cheese, an antioxidant-boosting mango and corn salsa, and protein-powered shrimp.

SERVES: 4
PREP: 5 MINS COOK: 1 HOUR

4 small sweet potatoes, scrubbed and
pricked with a fork
1/2 cup frozen corn kernels
2 plum tomatoes, cut into cubes
4 scallions, finely chopped
1 mango, pitted, peeled, and cut into cubes
1/3 cup finely chopped fresh cilantro
1 red chile, seeded and finely chopped (optional)
10 1/2 ounces cooked and peeled shrimp
finely grated zest and juice of 1 lime
1 1/4 cups low-fat cottage cheese
salt and pepper (optional)

1. Preheat the oven to 400°F. Put the sweet potatoes on a baking sheet and bake for 1 hour, or until they feel soft when gently squeezed.

2. Meanwhile, bring a saucepan of water to a boil, add the frozen corn kernels, and cook for 3 minutes, or until tender. Drain into a strainer, then rinse under cold running water.

3. Put the tomatoes, scallions, and mango in a bowl, then stir in the cilantro, red chile, if using, and corn kernels and season with salt and pepper, if using. Cover and chill in the refrigerator.

4. Put the shrimp and lime zest and juice in another bowl and season with salt and pepper, if using. Cover and chill in the refrigerator.

5. Put the sweet potatoes on a serving plate, slit them in half, then open them out. Top with spoonfuls of the cottage cheese, then fill with the salsa and shrimp.

SUPER SCALLIONS
Scallions are small, immature plants of the onion family. Because they are leafy greens, they contain more plant-derived antioxidants and fiber than onions and shallots. They contain vitamins A and C, and the B vitamins, and they are a rich source of vitamin K.

PER SERVING: 407 CALS | 2.3G FAT | 0.7G SAT FAT | 73.4G CARBS | 27.2G SUGARS | 10.2G FIBER | 25.5G PROTEIN | 840MG SODIUM

QUINOA SALAD
WITH FENNEL AND ORANGE

*Fennel is known to be an effective diuretic and calms the stomach,
so it is a useful addition to any detox diet. It is delicious with zingy orange.*

SERVES: 4
PREP: 20 MINS   COOK: 15 MINS

3³/₄ cups vegetable stock
1¹/₃ cups quinoa, rinsed
3 oranges
1 fennel bulb, thinly sliced, green feathery tops
reserved and torn into small pieces
2 scallions, finely chopped
¹/₄ cup coarsely chopped fresh flat-leaf parsley

DRESSING
juice of ¹/₂ lemon
3 tablespoons virgin olive oil
pepper (optional)

1. Bring the stock to a boil in a saucepan, add the quinoa, and simmer for 10–12 minutes, or until the germs separate from the seeds. Drain off the stock and discard, then spoon the quinoa into a salad bowl and let cool.

2. Grate the zest from two of the oranges and put it in a screw-top jar. Cut the peel and pith away from all three oranges with a small serrated knife. Hold each one above a bowl and cut between the membranes to release the sections into the bowl. Squeeze the juice from the membranes into the screw-top jar.

3. Add the orange sections, fennel slices, scallions, and parsley to the quinoa.

4. To make the dressing, add the lemon juice and oil to the screw-top jar, season with pepper, if using, screw on the lid, and shake well. Drizzle the dressing over the salad and toss. Garnish with the feathery fennel tops and serve immediately.

NUTRITIOUS QUINOA
Quinoa, pronounced "keen-wa," contains all
eight essential amino acids, plus it's
rich in fiber and minerals and lower in carbs
than most grains.

PER SERVING: 388 CALS | 8.3G FAT | 1.9G SAT FAT | 54G CARBS | 11.6G SUGARS | 8.4G FIBER | 10G PROTEIN | 840MG SODIUM

ROASTED BEET AND SQUASH SALAD

This nutty-tasting whole-grain salad, topped with two superfoods—beet and squash—can be made the night before, chilled, then tossed with beet leaves when serving.

SERVES: 4
PREP: 25 MINS   COOK: 30 MINS

5 raw beets (about 1 pound), cut into cubes
3¼ cups butternut squash cubes
¼ cup virgin olive oil
½ cup long-grain brown rice
½ cup French red Camargue rice (available online), or another ½ cup long-grain brown rice
½ cup farro (emmer wheat) or pearl barley
4 cups baby beet leaves
salt and pepper (optional)

DRESSING

1 tablespoon flaxseed oil
2 tablespoons red wine vinegar
½ teaspoon smoked hot paprika
1 teaspoon fennel seeds, coarsely crushed
2 teaspoons tomato paste

1. Preheat the oven to 400°F. Put the beets and squash into a roasting pan, drizzle with half the olive oil, and season with salt and pepper, if using. Roast for 30 minutes, or until just tender.

2. Meanwhile, bring a large saucepan of water to a boil, add the brown rice, red Camargue rice, and farro, and cook for about 30 minutes, or according to the package directions, until the grains are tender. (Depending on the brand, one of the grains may need more cooking time then another; start with the grain that needs the longest cooking time, then add the others so they will have enough cooking time to be tender but not overcooked.) Drain and rinse, then transfer to a plate.

3. To make the dressing, put all the ingredients and the remaining 2 tablespoons of olive oil in a screw-top jar, season with salt and pepper, if using, screw on the lid, and shake well. Drizzle over the rice mixture, then toss gently together.

4. Spoon the roasted vegetables over the grains and let cool. Toss gently, then sprinkle with the beet leaves and serve immediately.

BEET BONANZA

Packed with vitamins, minerals, protein, energy-boosting carbs, and powerful antioxidants, beets are thought to help reduce the oxidation of LDL cholesterol, so reducing the risk of heart disease and stroke. They are also rich in potassium, folic acid, and iron.

PER SERVING: 505 CALS | 19.3G FAT | 2.5G SAT FAT | 75G CARBS | 10.7G SUGARS | 9G FIBER | 10G PROTEIN | 440MG SODIUM

SUPERGREEN SALAD

Supercharged with vitamins and minerals, this crisp green salad tastes delicious with the addition of creamy smooth avocado and crunchy toasted seeds.

SERVES: 4
PREP: 15 MINS   COOK: 5 MINS

2 tablespoons pumpkin seeds
2 tablespoons sunflower seeds
2 tablespoons sesame seeds
4 teaspoons tamari sauce or soy sauce
3½ cups broccoli florets
3 cups baby spinach
¾ cup thinly shredded kale
⅓ cup coarsely chopped fresh cilantro
2 avocados, pitted, peeled, and sliced
juice of 2 limes

DRESSING
3 tablespoons flaxseed oil
2 teaspoons honey
pepper (optional)

1. Place a skillet over high heat. Add the pumpkin, sunflower, and sesame seeds, cover, and dry-fry for 3–4 minutes, or until lightly toasted and beginning to pop, shaking the pan from time to time. Remove from the heat and stir in the tamari sauce.

2. Fill the bottom of a steamer halfway with water, bring to a boil, then put the broccoli in the steamer top, cover with a lid, and steam for 3–5 minutes, or until tender. Transfer to a salad bowl and add the spinach, kale, and cilantro.

3. Put the avocados and half the lime juice in a small bowl and toss well, then transfer to the salad bowl.

4. To make the dressing, put the remaining lime juice, the oil, honey, and a little pepper, if using, in a small bowl and whisk together with a fork. Sprinkle the toasted seeds over the salad and serve immediately with the dressing for pouring over the top.

GO GREEN
Spinach, kale, and broccoli contain beneficial phytochemicals that help to prevent carcinogens from damaging DNA and so help to protect against cancer. They are also rich in vitamins A and C, the B vitamins, and iron.

PER SERVING: 388 CALS | 32.8G FAT | 3.9G SAT FAT | 22.1G CARBS | 5G SUGARS | 10.7G FIBER | 9G PROTEIN | 360MG SODIUM

CRANBERRY AND RED CABBAGE COLESLAW

Forget about coleslaw coated in thick, high-calorie mayonnaise.
This version is tossed with a tangy orange and olive oil dressing
flavored with chia seeds and toasted walnuts.

SERVES: 4
PREP: 15 MINS COOK: 3 MINS

1½ cups thinly shredded red cabbage
1 carrot, shredded
1 cup cauliflower florets
1 red-skinned sweet, crisp apple, quartered,
cored, and thinly sliced
⅓ cup dried cranberries
1 cup alfalfa and sango radish sprouts

DRESSING
⅓ cup coarsely chopped walnuts
juice of 1 orange
¼ cup virgin olive oil
2 tablespoons chia seeds
salt and pepper (optional)

1. Put the red cabbage, carrot, and cauliflower into a salad bowl. Add the apple, dried cranberries, and sprouts and toss well.

2. To make the dressing, put the walnuts in a large skillet and toast for 2–3 minutes, or until just beginning to brown.

3. Put the orange juice, oil, and chia seeds in a small bowl, season with salt and pepper, if using, then stir in the hot walnuts. Pour the dressing over the salad and toss. Serve immediately or cover and chill in the refrigerator until needed.

HEALTHY CRANBERRIES
Cranberries are packed with antioxidants.
They are believed to help reduce inflammation
and to be a useful tool in the fight against
heart disease.

PER SERVING: 320 CALS | 23.2G FAT | 2.8G SAT FAT | 29.5G CARBS | 16G SUGARS | 9.3G FIBER | 4.9G PROTEIN | 320MG SODIUM

PORK MEDALLIONS WITH POMEGRANATE SALAD

Fresh herbs and jewel-like pomegranate give this nutritious salad a delicious Middle Eastern flavor.

SERVES: 4
PREP: 10 MINS   COOK: 30 MINS

¾ cup wheat berries
⅓ cup coarsely chopped fresh flat-leaf parsley
¾ cup thinly shredded kale
seeds of 1 pomegranate
1 tablespoon olive oil
4 (4½-ounce) pork medallions, visible fat removed
2 garlic cloves, finely chopped
salt and pepper (optional)

DRESSING
⅓ cup coarsely chopped walnuts
3 tablespoons virgin olive oil
1 tablespoon pomegranate molasses
juice of 1 lemon

1. Bring a medium saucepan of water to a boil. Add the wheat berries and simmer for 25–30 minutes, or according to package directions, until tender. Drain and rinse.

2. Meanwhile, to make the dressing, put the walnuts in a large skillet and toast for 2–3 minutes, or until just beginning to brown. Put the virgin olive oil, pomegranate molasses, and lemon juice into a small bowl and mix together with a fork. Season with salt and pepper, if using, and stir in the hot walnuts.

3. Mix together the parsley, kale, and pomegranate seeds in a large bowl.

4. Heat the olive oil in the skillet over medium heat. Add the pork and garlic, season with salt and pepper, if using, and cook for 10 minutes, turning halfway through, until browned and cooked. Cut into the center of one of the pork medallions; any juices that run out should be clear and piping hot with steam rising. Slice the pork into strips.

5. Add the wheat berries to the kale and gently toss. Transfer to a plate, pour the dressing over the grains and vegetables, then top with the pork and serve.

PREPARING POMEGRANATES
Cut through the hard outer casing of a pomegranate to reveal the closely packed ruby seeds that are rich in vitamins A, C, and E plus antioxidants. Break and flex the fruit to pop out the seeds, or turn upside down over a bowl and hit the rounded edge with a wooden spoon to knock them out.

PER SERVING: 540 CALS | 29.7G FAT | 5.2G SAT FAT | 37G CARBS | 4.5G SUGARS | 6.9G FIBER | 34.6G PROTEIN | 360MG SODIUM

JERK CHICKEN WITH PAPAYA AND AVOCADO SALSA

*Glazed chicken doesn't need to have a high-calorie coating,
as this flavor-packed Jamaican dry spice rub shows.*

SERVES: 4
PREP: 15 MINS   COOK: 35 MINS

2¼ pounds small chicken drumsticks, skinned
1 tablespoon olive oil
1 romaine lettuce, leaves separated and torn into pieces (optional)
3 cups baby spinach (optional)

JERK SPICE RUB
1 teaspoon allspice berries, crushed
1 teaspoon coriander seeds, crushed
1 teaspoon mild paprika
¼ teaspoon freshly grated nutmeg
1 tablespoon fresh thyme leaves
1 tablespoon black peppercorns, coarsely crushed
pinch of salt

PAPAYA AND AVOCADO SALSA
1 papaya, halved, seeded, peeled, and cut into cubes
2 large avocados, pitted, peeled, and cut into cubes
finely grated zest and juice of 1 lime
½ red chile, seeded and finely chopped
½ red onion, finely chopped
⅓ cup fresh cilantro, finely chopped
2 teaspoons chia seeds

1. Preheat the oven to 400°F. To make the jerk spice rub, mix together all the ingredients in a small bowl.

2. Slash each chicken drumstick two or three times with a knife, then put them in a roasting pan and drizzle with the oil. Sprinkle the spice mix over the chicken, then rub it in with your fingers, washing your hands well afterwards. Roast the chicken for 30–35 minutes, or until browned with piping hot juices that run clear with no sign of pink when the tip of a sharp knife is inserted into the thickest part of a drumstick.

3. Meanwhile, to make the salsa, put the papaya and avocados in a bowl, sprinkle with the lime zest and juice, then toss well. Add the chile, red onion, cilantro, and chia seeds and stir.

4. Toss the lettuce and spinach together, if using. Serve with the chicken and salsa.

THREE CHEERS FOR CHIA
Chia is a good source of omega–3 fats and fiber, and it contains calcium, manganese, and phosphorus. It is thought to have many health benefits, including providing energy, stabilizing blood sugar, aiding digestion, and lowering cholesterol.

PER SERVING: 394 CALS | 18.1G FAT | 3.2G SAT FAT | 17.1G CARBS | 5.4G SUGARS | 7.8G FIBER | 42G PROTEIN | 360MG SODIUM

SPICY ROASTED TURKEY

This easy one-dish meal makes a healthy midweek dinner—with little dishwashing required.

SERVES: 4
PREP: 20 MINS   COOK: 45 MINS

3 tablespoons olive oil
½ butternut squash or other squash (about 1 pound),
seeded, peeled, and cut into large pieces
3 sweet potatoes, cut into large pieces
7 ounces baby carrots, tops trimmed, larger ones
halved lengthwise
1 small cauliflower, cut into large florets
1 pound skinless and boneless turkey breast,
cut into ½-inch-thick slices
salt and pepper (optional)

SPICE BLEND
2 tablespoons sesame seeds
2 tablespoons sunflower seeds
2 teaspoons mild paprika
1 teaspoon coriander seeds, crushed
1 teaspoon fennel seeds, crushed
1 teaspoon cumin seeds, crushed

1. Preheat the oven to 400°F. To make the spice blend, mix all the ingredients together in a small bowl and season with salt and pepper, if using.

2. Pour the oil into a large roasting pan, then heat in the oven for 1 minute. Put the squash, sweet potatoes, and carrots in the roasting pan and toss in the hot oil. Roast for 15 minutes.

3. Add the cauliflower to the roasting pan and turn all the vegetables so they are coated in the oil. Push them to the edges of the pan, then add the turkey in a single layer.

4. Sprinkle the spice blend over the turkey and vegetables, then turn the vegetables so they are evenly coated. Roast for 20–25 minutes, or until the vegetables are tender and the turkey is golden brown with piping hot juices that run clear with no sign of pink when the thickest slice is cut in half.

5. Spoon the turkey and vegetables onto plates and serve immediately.

TALKING TURKEY
Turkey is a rich source of protein, but is low in fat. It also contains iron, zinc, potassium, and phosphorus, as well as vitamin B₆ and niacin, which are essential for the body's energy production.

PER SERVING: 455 CALS | 16.6G FAT | 2.3G SAT FAT | 45.5G CARBS | 11G SUGARS | 9.8G FIBER | 34.2G PROTEIN | 440MG SODIUM

TANGY TURKEY MEATBALLS WITH EDAMAME

Ground turkey breast can be quickly processed with lemon and garlic to make this simple midweek dinner that's superhealthy, low in fat, and high in protein.

SERVES: 4
PREP: 20 MINS   COOK: 30 MINS

1¼ cups short-grain brown rice
1 small onion, coarsely chopped
1 slice of whole-wheat bread, torn into pieces
2 garlic cloves, thinly sliced
1 pound ground turkey breast
finely grated zest of 1 unwaxed lemon
1 tablespoon olive oil
1½ cups chicken stock
1 cup frozen edamame
¾ cup peas
2 egg yolks
¼ cup coarsely chopped fresh flat-leaf parsley
⅓ cup coarsely chopped fresh mint
salt and pepper (optional)

1. Cook the rice in a large saucepan of lightly salted boiling water for 30 minutes, or according to the package directions, until tender. Drain well.

2. Meanwhile, put the onion, bread, and garlic in a food processor and process until finely chopped. Add the turkey and lemon zest and season with salt and pepper, if using, then process again briefly until mixed.

3. Spoon the mixture into 20 mounds, then shape them into balls using wet hands.

4. Heat the oil in a large lidded skillet over medium heat. Add the meatballs in a single layer and cook for 15 minutes, or until evenly browned, turning from time to time.

5. Add the stock, cover, and cook for 5 minutes. Add the edamame and peas, replace the lid, and cook for 5 minutes, or until the vegetables are just tender and the meatballs are cooked through with juices that are piping hot and that run clear with no sign of pink when a meatball is cut in half. Remove from the heat and spoon the stock into a bowl.

6. Meanwhile, whisk the egg yolks together in a large bowl and season with salt and pepper, if using. Gradually whisk in the stock until smooth, then pour the mixture back into the pan. Place over low heat and cook, stirring all the time, for 3–4 minutes, or until thickened. Be careful not to have the heat too high or the egg yolks will scramble.

7. Stir in the herbs. Spoon the rice into shallow bowls, top with the meatballs and sauce, and serve immediately.

BEAUTIFUL BROWN RICE
Brown rice is unrefined, so it still has the hull and bran, making it rich in fiber, the B vitamins, magnesium, and potassium.

PER SERVING: 546 CALS | 11.8G FAT | 2.4G SAT FAT | 62.4G CARBS | 3.4G SUGARS | 6.5G FIBER | 45G PROTEIN | 720MG SODIUM

RISOTTO PRIMAVERA

Short-grain brown rice adds a delicious nutty taste to risotto.
It's high in fiber and is believed to help lower cholesterol.

SERVES: 4
PREP: 20 MINS   COOK: 50 MINS

5 cups vegetable stock
1 tablespoon olive oil
1 large leek, thinly sliced, white and green slices kept separate
2 garlic cloves, finely chopped
¼ cup short-grain brown rice
5½ ounces baby carrots, tops trimmed, halved lengthwise
6 asparagus spears, woody stems removed
1 zucchini, cut into cubes
2 tablespoons butter
¾ cup finely grated fresh Parmesan cheese
2¼ cups mixed baby spinach, watercress, and arugula leaves

1. Bring the stock to a boil in a saucepan.

2. Meanwhile, heat the oil in a large skillet over medium heat. Add the white leek slices and garlic and cook for 3–4 minutes, or until softened but not browned.

3. Stir in the rice and cook for 1 minute. Pour in half the hot stock, bring back to a boil, then cover and simmer for 15 minutes.

4. Add the carrots and half the remaining stock and stir again. Cover and cook for 15 minutes.

5. Add the green leek slices, asparagus, and zucchini, then add a little extra stock. Replace the lid and cook for 5–6 minutes, or until the vegetables and rice are just tender.

6. Remove from the heat, stir in the butter and two-thirds of the cheese, and add a little more stock, if needed. Top with the mixed salad greens, cover with the lid, and warm through for 1–2 minutes, or until the leaves just begin to wilt.

7. Spoon into shallow bowls, sprinkle with the remaining cheese, and serve immediately.

LOVELY LEEKS

Leeks are part of the onion family and contain many antioxidants, minerals, and vitamins, including folic acid, niacin, riboflavin, and thiamin. They are a good source of vitamin A as well as containing vitamins C, E, and K.

PER SERVING: 474 CALS | 17G FAT | 8.1G SAT FAT | 69.4G CARBS | 8.1G SUGARS | 6.4G FIBER | 14.6G PROTEIN | 1,520MG SODIUM

CHOCOLATE, CINNAMON, AND VANILLA CUSTARD DESSERTS

Rich, dark, and smooth, these easy-to-make desserts not only look fabulous but will also satisfy any chocolate craving.

MAKES: 6 DESSERTS
PREP: 20 MINS   COOK: 50 MINS   CHILL: 5 HOURS

2 cups low-fat milk
7 ounces semisweet chocolate (at least 65 percent cocoa solids), broken into pieces, plus 1 tablespoon finely grated semisweet chocolate to decorate
1 teaspoon vanilla extract
¼ teaspoon ground cinnamon
¼ cup honey
2 eggs, plus 2 egg yolks
⅓ cup fat-free Greek-style plain yogurt, to decorate

1. Preheat the oven to 300°F. Pour the milk into a heavy saucepan, bring just to a boil, then remove from the heat and stir in the chocolate pieces, vanilla extract, ground cinnamon, and 3 tablespoons of honey. Set aside for 5 minutes, or until the chocolate has melted. Stir until the milk is an even dark chocolate color.

2. Put the eggs and egg yolks into a large bowl and beat lightly with a fork. Gradually pour in the warm chocolate milk, beating all the time with a wooden spoon, until smooth. Strain back into the saucepan through a strainer, then press any remaining chocolate through the strainer using the back of the spoon.

3. Put six ¾-cup ovenproof teacups or ramekins (ceramic dishes) into a roasting pan. Fill the cups with the chocolate mixture, then pour hot water into the roasting pan to reach halfway up the cups. Cover the cups with aluminum foil, then bake for 40–45 minutes, or until the custards are just set, with a slight wobble in the center.

4. Using oven mitts, lift the cups out of the roasting pan and let cool, then cover with plastic wrap and chill in the refrigerator for 4–5 hours.

5. Place the cups on a serving plate, remove the plastic wrap, and top each with a spoonful of yogurt, a drizzle of the remaining honey, and a little grated chocolate.

DARK CHOCOLATE IS GOOD FOR YOU!

Research shows that dark chocolate is packed with antioxidants and may help lower blood pressure, but it must have 65 percent or ideally more cocoa content. The darker it is, the less fat and sugar it will probably contain.

PER CUP: 343 CALS | 19.5G FAT | 10.6G SAT FAT | 32.3G CARBS | 24.5G SUGARS | 3.8G FIBER | 10G PROTEIN | 80MG SODIUM

SKINNY BANANA SPLIT SUNDAES

Keep this twist on a traditional sundae in the freezer, then make the chocolate sauce just before serving, for a superfood-packed standby dessert everyone will love.

SERVES: 2

PREP: 10 MINS   COOK: 6 MINS   FREEZE: 3 HOURS

2 small bananas, peeled and coarsely chopped
6 unblanched almonds, coarsely chopped

CHOCOLATE SAUCE
2 tablespoons packed light brown sugar
3 tablespoons unsweetened cocoa powder
⅓ cup plus 1 tablespoon low-fat milk
1 ounce bittersweet chocolate (at least 70 percent cocoa solids), broken into pieces
½ teaspoon vanilla extract

1. Put the bananas into a plastic container and freeze for 2 hours. Transfer to a food processor and process until smooth and creamy. Return to the container, replace the lid, and freeze for 1 hour, or until firm.

2. To make the chocolate sauce, put the sugar, cocoa powder, and milk into a small saucepan and bring to a simmer over medium heat. Reduce the heat to low and cook, stirring constantly, for 1 minute, or until the sugar and cocoa powder have dissolved.

3. Remove from the heat, then stir in the chocolate until it has melted. Stir in the vanilla extract. Let cool slightly.

4. Place a skillet over high heat. Add the almonds, cover, and dry-fry for 3–4 minutes, or until toasted.

5. Scoop the banana puree into two glasses or bowls, drizzle with the warm chocolate sauce, and sprinkle with the almonds.

AMAZING ALMONDS
Almonds are a rich source of calcium, protein, essential fats, the B vitamins, and vitamin E. They also contain iron, potassium, and magnesium, as well as copper, which is needed in red blood cell production and so can help prevent anemia.

PER SERVING: 311 CALS | 11.3G FAT | 5.1G SAT FAT | 52.9G CARBS | 33.7G SUGARS | 7.5G FIBER | 6.4G PROTEIN | TRACE SODIUM

WARM WALNUT AND ORANGE CAKE

A Middle Eastern-inspired cake that is gluten-free and packed with energy-boosting nuts. The whole cooked orange gives it a tangy, high-fiber citrus hit.

MAKES: 10 SLICES
PREP: 25 MINS   COOK: 2¾ HOURS

3 large whole oranges
1 cup dried apricots
⅔ cup coarsely chopped walnuts,
plus 12 halves to decorate
¾ cup unblanched almonds, coarsely chopped,
plus 6 to decorate
½ cup Brazil nuts, coarsely chopped,
plus 12 to decorate
4 eggs
1 cup superfine or granulated sugar
½ cup light olive oil, plus extra to grease
½ cup brown rice flour
2 teaspoons baking powder
1 cup fat-free Greek-style plain yogurt, to serve

BRILLIANT BRAZIL NUTS
Brazil nuts are a good source of the mineral selenium, which we need to produce the active thyroid hormone, and which helps boost your immune system. They are also rich in protein and fiber.

1. Put one orange in a small saucepan, just cover with water, then bring to a boil, cover, and simmer for 45 minutes. Add the dried apricots, replace the lid, and cook for 15 minutes, or until the orange is tender when pierced with a knife. Drain the fruits, reserving the cooking water, and let cool.

2. Preheat the oven to 325°F. Lightly brush a 9½-inch round springform cake pan with a little oil. Put the measured walnuts, almonds, and Brazil nuts into a food processor and process until finely ground. Transfer to a large mixing bowl.

3. Coarsely chop the cooked orange, discard any seeds, then put it and the apricots in a food processor and process into a coarse puree. Add the eggs, ¾ cup of sugar, and all the oil, and process again until smooth.

4. Spoon the brown rice flour and baking powder into the ground nuts and mix well. Transfer to the food processor and process briefly until smooth. Pour the cake batter into the prepared pan, spread it level with a spatula, and decorate with the walnut halves, whole almonds, and whole Brazil nuts.

5. Bake for 1–1¼ hours, or until browned, slightly cracked on top, and a toothpick inserted into the center comes out clean. Check after 40 minutes and loosely cover the top with aluminum foil if the nut decoration is browning too quickly.

6. Cut the peel and pith away from the remaining oranges with a small serrated knife. Cut between the membranes to release the sections. Measure ½ cup of the reserved orange cooking water, making it up with extra water, if needed, and pour it into a small saucepan. Add the remaining sugar and cook over low heat until the sugar has dissolved. Increase the heat to high and boil for 3 minutes, or until you have a syrup. Add the orange sections and let cool.

7. Loosen the edge of the cake with a blunt knife and turn out onto a wire rack. Let cool slightly, then cut into wedges and serve warm, with the oranges in syrup and spoonfuls of the Greek yogurt.

PER SLICE: 517 CALS | 33.7G FAT | 5.3G SAT FAT | 47.4G CARBS | 34.6G SUGARS | 5.2G FIBER | 11.9G PROTEIN | 320MG SODIUM

BROILED PEACHES AND NECTARINES

When you need a glamorous dessert but you're in a rush, this low-fat treat bursting with fresh fruit is just the thing.

SERVES: 6
PREP: 10 MINS   COOK: 5 MINS

1½ cups low-fat ricotta cheese
2 teaspoons finely grated orange zest
3 peaches, pitted and quartered
3 nectarines, pitted and quartered
3 plums or apricots, pitted and quartered
2 tablespoons honey, ideally orange blossom
2 tablespoons slivered almonds

1. Preheat the broiler to medium-high. Line the broiler rack with aluminum foil.

2. Put the ricotta and orange zest in a bowl and stir well.

3. Lay all the fruit in a single layer on the foil-lined broiler rack. Broil the fruit, turning halfway, for 5 minutes, or until softened and beginning to caramelize.

4. Spoon the ricotta into six glasses. Top each with some broiled fruit, drizzle with the honey, and sprinkle with the slivered almonds. Serve immediately.

REACH FOR APRICOTS

Apricots are rich in beta-carotene, which is important for vision, and vitamin C. They are also a good source of fiber and minerals, such as potassium and manganese.

PER SERVING: 202 CALS | 7.1G FAT | 3.2G SAT FAT | 28.1G CARBS | 21.2G SUGARS | 3.2G FIBER | 9.5G PROTEIN | 80MG SODIUM

GREEN TEA FRUIT SALAD

The delicate and refreshing taste of green tea works well mixed with chopped fresh mint and a hint of honey in a syrup for a fruit salad.

SERVES: 4
PREP: 15 MINS   CHILL: 1 HOUR

2 teaspoons green tea
1 cup boiling water
1 tablespoon honey
½ small watermelon, seeded, peeled, and cut into cubes
1 large mango, pitted, peeled, and cut into cubes
1 papaya, seeded, peeled, and cut into cubes
2 pears, peeled, cored, and cut into cubes
2 kiwis, peeled and cut into cubes
2 tablespoons coarsely chopped fresh mint
seeds of ½ pomegranate
2 tablespoons coarsely chopped pistachio nuts

1. Put the tea into a teapot or saucepan, pour boiling water over the leaves, and let brew for 3–4 minutes. Strain into a small bowl, stir in the honey, and let cool.

2. Put the watermelon, mango, and papaya into a large serving bowl, then add the pears, kiwis, and mint. Pour the cooled green tea over the fruits and stir gently.

3. Cover the fruit salad with plastic wrap and chill in the refrigerator for 1 hour. Stir gently to mix the tea through the fruits.

4. Spoon the fruit salad into four bowls and serve sprinkled with the pomegranate seeds and pistachio nuts.

GO FOR GREEN TEA
Green tea is used in traditional Chinese medicine. It contains antioxidants, and is thought to have antibacterial and antiviral properties.

PER SERVING: 313 CALS | 4.8G FAT | 0.6G SAT FAT | 70.8G CARBS | 54G SUGARS | 10G FIBER | 5.2G PROTEIN | TRACE SODIUM

CLEAN EATING

WHAT IS CLEAN EATING?

Clean eating means eating foods in their most natural, whole state, thereby maximizing their nutritional benefits. In the last ten years, the space supermarkets devote to prepared chilled meals has expanded greatly, and the shelf life of some so-called "fresh" foods has been unnaturally extended, but at what cost? Foods often contain long lists of strange-sounding ingredients that are difficult to pronounce and with roles that are unclear. Bread may no longer contain just flour, yeast, sugar, salt, and water; it often includes a number of other ingredients. As increasing evidence emerges about the dangers of eating processed food, clean eating tries to sidestep the problem by going natural.

Clean eating involves eating cleaner, leaner meats and more fish, low-starch vegetables, vitamin-rich fruits, protein-boosting nuts, and mineral-rich seeds. You are encouraged to replace refined carbohydrates with smart, complex carbs in the form of legumes and whole grains, because they take more time to digest, leaving you feeling full for longer while sustaining your blood sugar levels.

Clean eating doesn't mean focusing on calorie restriction; it's about enjoying food as close to "as nature intended" as possible, avoiding refined processed foods and artificial chemicals, flavors, and preservatives, and replacing them with foods grown locally, in a sustainable and environmentally friendly way. You are encouraged to eat foods that are ethically produced, so, for example, choosing eggs from cage-free hens.

The first step is to look at what you buy and get label-savvy. Food packaging can give a false impression of what is healthy, and words such as "whole grain," "reduced-sugar," or "high-fiber" may not tell the whole story, even when they are printed alongside pictures of fresh vegetables, green fields, waterfalls, and well-cared-for livestock.

Turn the package over and you may be surprised at what is in the food. Ingredients are listed in order, with those included in the largest amount listed first, and the ingredient you expect to come first may be far down the list. Say "no" to high-fructose corn syrup, hydrogenated oils, mechanically separated chicken, MSG, sodium nitrates, and a high sodium content.

Cutting out processed food can feel like a big transition, but as with any dietary change, the hardest part is making the decision. You can still enjoy a burger; choose a homemade one made with good organic lean beef (see page 80); it will taste better than the store-bought alternatives. This is a sustainable, proactive approach to healthy living that will see you enjoying what you eat and leave you feeling revitalized.

WHAT YOU CAN EAT

The best way to improve your diet is to start cooking your food from scratch—that way you will know exactly what's in it, including the provenance of the ingredients and how it has been prepared. Fresh food served straight from the oven should contain no horrible chemicals to enhance its shelf life, especially if you use organic ingredients where possible. You may also be surprised to find that it can save you money, particularly when you have to cook for a family.

CHOOSE WHOLE GRAINS

Whole grains help to maintain a healthy digestive system and aid good heart health, because the high amounts of soluble fiber help to reduce cholesterol. They are also rich in complex carbohydrates, for a slow and sustained energy release to help reduce tiredness.

Switching from refined white bread to whole wheat is arguably the single best change you can make to your diet. Wheat flour that is sold as "whole wheat" refers to the whole grain that is ground, with nothing taken away during milling, leaving you with 75 percent flour, 23 percent bran, and 2 percent wheat germ. You might also like to try whole-grain spelt or kamut flour, both of which are ancient varieties of wheat, or brown rice, hemp, quinoa, or buckwheat flour for a gluten-free alternative.

Check the label of any flour carefully. What you think is whole grain may actually be a mix of refined white wheat flour and whole-wheat flour, or even solely refined white flour with whole seeds, grains, or flakes added. Some flours might be refined white flour with 10–15 percent fine or coarse bran put back in after the milling process.

Wheat is also available in its whole-grain form as wheat berries, which can be used as a nutty-tasting salad base and make a great alternative to brown rice. Also try cracked or bulgur wheat, which cooks in less time than wheat berries and is a great base for Middle Eastern salads. Enjoy whole-grain couscous or whole-wheat pasta as a hot side dish in place of white couscous or pasta. Oats are always sold in their whole-grain form, either as rolled oats or instant oats. They are also available as groats, which look similar to wheat berries and can be cooked in the same way. Look for barley groats and barley flakes, too. When buying rice, choose whole-grain brown rice or colored rice, such as Camargue red rice or black wild rice. White rice not only has the fiber removed, but most of the B vitamins are lost in the processing, too. Also choose whole-grain corn flour or cornmeal.

FISH AND MEAT

Fish is rich in protein, vitamin B12, which is vital for a healthy nervous system, and iodine, which the thyroid gland needs to function effectively. Oily fish, such as salmon, trout, fresh tuna, sardines, herring, and mackerel, are rich in omega-3 fats, which are thought to have many health benefits, including helping to lower blood pressure.

Don't be afraid to ask your fish dealer where the fish has come from, how it was caught, and whether it is farmed or wild. Look for the Marine Stewardship Council (MSC) logo, which certifies that the fish has been sourced from well-managed fisheries, where fishing methods minimize environmental impact so we can be confident of healthy fish stocks in the future.

When buying meat and poultry, ask your butcher about its provenance and choose farms with high welfare standards. Try to have at least two meat-free days per week, and try to keep portions small; check government guidelines for latest advice. Trim the fat off meat before cooking and remove the skin from poultry before eating.

FATS AND OILS

We need fat in the diet to help the body absorb fat-soluble vitamins A, D, E, and K and to provide essential fatty acids. The Mediterranean diet, rich in olive oil, has long been considered to be healthy, but there is now a wide range of other cold-pressed oils, such as hemp, avocado, and nut oils, available in some supermarkets.

They are traditionally made without the use of chemicals or solvents, and at temperatures below 104° F, which makes sure the full character and essence of the oil is preserved, with natural variations in character and appearance from season to season.

Nearly all cold-pressed oils are a natural source of vitamin E, which is an important cancer-fighting antioxidant, plus they contain essential fatty acids 3 and 6. Many cold-pressed oils, such as flaxseed and walnut oils, keep less well than refined oils, so buy them in small quantities and keep them in a cool place or in the refrigerator.

Butter contains saturated fat, so use it sparingly—check government guidelines for the latest advice on portion sizes per day. Make dips and dressings with yogurt instead of store-bought mayonnaise.

FRUIT AND VEGETABLES

What counts as a portion of fruit or vegetables? A medium fruit, such as an apple, pear, or banana, counts as one, as do two kiwis or plums or seven strawberries. Potatoes don't count, but sweet potatoes and other starchy vegetables do. While fresh is generally considered best, frozen fruit and vegetables can sometimes contain more vitamins and minerals than fresh, plus they have the benefit of being convenient and are ideal for smoothies and compotes. Canned tomatoes or beans, such as great northern or red kidney beans, in water make a great pantry standby and count toward your daily quota.

Try to choose organically farmed local produce grown by traditional crop rotation methods using natural pesticides and fertilizers from your local farmers' market. Some supermarkets also support local producers and will label food accordingly. Or why not try growing your own? You don't need a large yard; just convert the end of a flower bed or grow salad greens in containers, or have a hanging basket of strawberries by the back door. There's something immensely satisfying about harvesting your own food, and it's a great way to encourage children to be more interested in where their food comes from.

Most pesticides on the surface of fruit and vegetables can be removed with thorough washing. Choose unwaxed lemons, but buy them in small quantities, because one benefit of the wax is it contains a fungicide to prevent mold growth.

UNREFINED SUGARS

Most of us eat far too much sugar, and with high obesity levels, it is good to review what you eat. Instead of grabbing a chocolate bar packed with chemically derived sugars for a quick fix, go for a homemade cupcake with whole-wheat flour for a more sustained energy boost (see page 92).

If using sugar, choose types that are as unrefined as possible; naturally brown unbleached sugars work well, but check the package to make sure the sugars aren't colored after manufacture. Maple syrup adds a delicate natural sweetness, but again it may not be all that it seems; check the label, because some brands are mixed with high-fructose corn syrup. Locally produced honey tastes delicious, and a small spoonful goes a long way.

KEEP IT SIMPLE

The recipes in this chapter are simple, approachable, and made with raw, natural ingredients that are easy to find in your favorite supermarket or health food store. Here are just some of the problems you can help avoid if you switch to clean eating.

HIGH SODIUM INTAKE

Even if you don't add salt to your food, you may still be consuming far too much sodium if you eat processed foods, such as breakfast cereals and canned soups, not to mention potato chips and other snacks.

HIGH FRUCTOSE LEVELS

Health-care workers fear that the high level of fructose in our diet is set to become as great a problem as our alcohol consumption. Avoid sugary processed foods and fruit juices, as well as soft drinks with little or no added nutritional benefit.

HIGH TRANS FAT CONSUMPTION

These are naturally found in meat and dairy products, but they are also artificially produced to go into some cookies and cakes, with edible oils being industrially hardened to make sure they stay solid at room temperature. It is the artificially made trans fats that should be avoided.

ZUCCHINI FRITTERS

Quick to prepare, these fritters make a filling start to the day. Brown rice flour is a nutritious alternative to wheat flour and is gluten-free.

SERVES: 5
PREP: 20 MINS   COOK: 40 MINS

½ cup brown rice flour
1 teaspoon baking powder
2 eggs, beaten
1 cup milk
1 medium-large zucchini
2 tablespoons fresh thyme leaves
1 tablespoon virgin olive oil
sea salt and pepper (optional)

1. Sift the flour and baking powder into a large bowl, then tip the remaining bran in the sifter into the bowl. Make a well in the center. Pour the eggs into the well and, using a wooden spoon, gradually draw in the flour. Slowly pour in the milk, stirring continuously to form a thick batter.

2. Place paper towels on a plate and shred the zucchini over it so the paper absorbs some of the juices. Pat the zucchini dry, then add it and the thyme to the batter, season with salt and pepper, if using, and mix well.

3. Heat the oil in a skillet over medium–high heat. Drop tablespoons of the batter into the pan, leaving a little space between them. Cook in batches for 3–4 minutes on each side, or until golden brown.

4. Line a baking sheet with paper towels. Transfer the fritters to the baking sheet, using a slotted spoon, and let them drain well. Remove the paper towels and keep each batch warm while you make the rest. Allow five fritters per person and serve immediately.

SPICE IT UP
These fritters are delicious with a large pinch of dried crushed red pepper flakes mixed in with the salt and pepper.

PER SERVING: 151 CALS | 6.8G FAT | 2G SAT FAT | 16.6G CARBS | 3.5G SUGARS | 1.3G FIBER | 5.9G PROTEIN | 560MG SODIUM

BUCKWHEAT BLINIS WITH PEARS AND BLUEBERRIES

These Russian-style pancakes were traditionally served to mark the coming of spring, and are made with nutritious and nutty-tasting buckwheat flour.

SERVES: 4

PREP: 25 MINS   RISE: 1 HOUR   COOK: 25 MINS

1¹⁄₃ cups buckwheat flour
½ teaspoon sea salt
2 teaspoons packed dark brown sugar
1 teaspoon active dry yeast
½ cup milk
½ cup water
1 tablespoon virgin olive oil

TOPPING
2 tablespoons unsalted butter
2 Bosc pears, cored and thickly sliced
1 cup blueberries
2 tablespoons honey
juice of ½ lemon
1 cup plain Greek-style yogurt
pinch of ground cinnamon
¼ cup toasted unblanched hazelnuts, coarsely chopped

1. To make the blinis, put the flour, salt, sugar, and yeast into a large bowl and mix well. Put the milk and water into a small saucepan and gently heat until warm, then gradually whisk into the flour until you have a smooth, thick batter.

2. Cover the bowl with a large plate and let rest in a warm place to rise for 40–60 minutes, or until bubbles appear on the surface and the batter is almost doubled in size.

3. Heat half the oil in a large griddle pan or skillet over medium heat. Remove the pan from the heat briefly and wipe away excess oil, using paper towels. Return the pan to the heat and drop tablespoons of the batter into it, leaving a little space between them. Cook for 2–3 minutes, or until the undersides are golden and the tops are beginning to bubble.

4. Turn the blinis over with a spatula and cook for another 1–2 minutes. Transfer them to a baking sheet and keep warm in the oven while you make the rest. Continue wiping the pan with oiled paper towels between cooking batches.

5. To make the topping, melt the butter in a skillet over medium heat. Add the fruit and cook for 2–3 minutes, or until hot. Drizzle with the honey and lemon juice and cook for 1 minute, or until the blueberry juices begin to run.

6. Arrange three blinis on each of four plates and top with spoonfuls of the yogurt, the hot fruit, a little ground cinnamon, and the hazelnuts. Serve immediately.

GLUTEN-FREE FLOUR
Buckwheat flour is ground from a plant related to rhubarb. It is gluten-free, but check the label; it may be milled by machines used for wheat, making it unsuitable for those on a gluten-free diet.

PER SERVING: 437 CALS | 17.4G FAT | 6.6G SAT FAT | 63.8G CARBS | 26.6G SUGARS | 8.5G FIBER | 12.9G PROTEIN | 360MG SODIUM

SPELT BREAKFAST ROLLS WITH SPICED FIG CONSERVE

What could be nicer than starting the day with home-baked bread?
This quick-cook fig conserve is a great way to make your own spread at home, too.

MAKES: 16 ROLLS AND 2 CUPS OF CONSERVE
PREP: 45 MINS   RISE: OVERNIGHT PLUS 50 MINS
COOK: 45 MINS

4 cups whole-grain spelt flour,
plus extra to dust
1 tablespoon packed dark brown sugar
1 teaspoon sea salt
2 teaspoons active dry yeast
2 tablespoons sesame seeds, plus extra to sprinkle
2 tablespoons sunflower seeds, plus extra to sprinkle
2 tablespoons flaxseed, plus extra to sprinkle
2 tablespoons virgin olive oil, plus extra to grease
1 1/4–1 1/2 cups warm water
1 teaspoon milk, to glaze
unsalted butter, to serve

SPICED FIG CONSERVE
1 cup diced dried figs
3 small McIntosh, Gala, or other sweet, crisp apples,
peeled, quartered, cored, and diced
finely grated zest and juice of 1 orange
1 tablespoon packed light brown sugar
1/4 teaspoon ground allspice
1 cup water

1. Put the flour, dark brown sugar, and salt in a bowl and mix well. Stir in the yeast, sesame seeds, sunflower seeds, and flaxseed. Add the oil, then gradually mix in enough warm water to create a soft dough, at first using a wooden spoon, then squeezing together with your hands.

2. Dust a work surface with spelt flour, then knead the dough for 5 minutes. Return it to the bowl, cover with lightly oiled plastic wrap, and let rise overnight in the refrigerator.

3. Meanwhile, to make the spiced fig conserve, put the dried figs, apples, orange zest and juice, light brown sugar, allspice, and water into a saucepan. Cover and simmer over medium heat, stirring from time to time, for 30 minutes, or until thick. Let cool. Spoon the conserve into a sterilized jar, then let stand until completely cold. Store in the refrigerator for up to ten days.

4. Line two baking sheets with parchment paper. Dust a work surface with more spelt flour. Knead the dough briefly, then cut it into 16 pieces. Roll each piece into a ball, put one ball in the center of each baking sheet, then arrange the others around it, leaving a little space between them.

5. Cover each baking sheet of rolls with lightly oiled plastic wrap and let rise in a warm place for 40–50 minutes. Preheat the oven to 425°F. Remove the plastic wrap, brush the rolls with the milk, and sprinkle with the remaining seeds. Bake for 15 minutes, or until the rolls are browned and sound hollow when tapped underneath. Serve with butter and the conserve.

TO STERILIZE JARS
Sterilize the jar in a dishwasher.
Follow USDA guidelines for heating
in a hot water bath for longer storage.

PER ROLL (NO CONSERVE): 199 CALS | 4.4G FAT | 0.5G SAT FAT | 37.5G CARBS | 13.5G SUGARS | 6G FIBER | 6G PROTEIN | 160MG SODIUM

CITRUS FRUIT REFRESHER

You can quickly put this together in the morning, or make it the night before and chill it in the refrigerator in a sealed plastic container so it's ready and waiting for you.

SERVES: 4
PREP: 20 MINS

1 ruby grapefruit
1 pink grapefruit
2 oranges
1 honeydew melon, halved, seeded, peeled,
and cut into chunks
finely grated zest and juice of 1 lime
½ cup finely shredded fresh mint
2 tablespoons honey

1. Cut the peel and pith away from the grapefruits and oranges with a small serrated knife. Hold one of the fruits above a bowl and cut between the membranes to release the sections. Squeeze the juice from the membranes into the bowl. Continue until the fruits have all been sectioned.

2. Add the melon, lime zest and juice, and half the mint. Drizzle with the honey, then gently stir with a large spoon. Decorate with the remaining mint and serve.

GROWING MINT
Mint is such a prolific herb that just one packet of seeds in a large flowerpot will usually provide enough for the whole summer.

PER SERVING: 170 CALS | 0.5G FAT | 0.1G SAT FAT | 43.6G CARBS | 35G SUGARS | 4.9G FIBER | 2.3G PROTEIN | TRACE SODIUM

BERRY KICK-START SMOOTHIE

*This energizing, gorgeous-looking smoothie is a delicious
and healthy way to kick-start your day.*

SERVES: 2
PREP: 10 MINS

1¼ cups blueberries
1¼ cups cranberries
²/₃ cup plain yogurt
2 teaspoon honey
¼ cup cold water

1. Put the blueberries and cranberries into a blender and process until smooth.

2. Add the yogurt, honey, and water and process again. Pour into a glass and serve.

THE BUZZ ABOUT HONEY

Honey supplies energy in the form of simple carbohydrates, and is a mixture of fructose and glucose. Sweet foods stimulate the brain to produce endorphins, the body's natural painkillers. Agave syrup, brown rice syrup, and date syrup can all be used instead of honey. Agave syrup is naturally sweeter than honey. Brown rice syrup has a mild caramel flavor and tastes similar to maple syrup. Date syrup is a thick, concentrated puree of lightly cooked dates; you can make it by gently simmering dates with a little water, cinnamon, and vanilla, then pureeing.

PER SERVING: 288 CALS | 5.6G FAT | 3.1G SAT FAT | 57.9G CARBS | 40.5G SUGARS | 9.5G FIBER | 6.9G PROTEIN | 40MG SODIUM

FAVA BEAN AND MINT HUMMUS WITH VEGETABLE STICKS

This summery hummus, made with freshly shelled fava beans flavored with chopped fresh herbs and lemon juice, is delicious on warm homemade pita bread.

SERVES: 4
PREP: 25 MINS   COOK: 10 MINS

2⅓ cups shelled fava beans
2 tablespoons virgin olive oil
1 teaspoon cumin seeds, crushed
3 scallions, thinly sliced
2 garlic cloves, finely chopped
½ cup fresh mint, torn into pieces
½ cup finely chopped fresh flat-leaf parsley
juice of 1 lemon
⅓ cup Greek-style plain yogurt
sea salt and pepper (optional)

TO SERVE
1 red and 1 yellow bell pepper, seeded and cut into sticks
4 celery stalks, cut into sticks
½ cucumber, halved, seeded, and cut into sticks
pita bread (optional)

1. Fill the bottom of a steamer halfway with water, bring to a boil, then put the beans in the steamer top, cover with a lid, and steam for 10 minutes, or until tender.

2. Meanwhile, heat the oil in a skillet over medium heat. Add the cumin, scallions, and garlic and cook for 2 minutes, or until the scallions are softened.

3. Put the beans in a food processor or blender, add the scallion mixture, herbs, lemon juice, and yogurt, and season with a little salt and pepper, if using. Process to a coarse puree, then spoon into a dish set on a large plate.

4. Arrange the vegetable sticks around the hummus and serve with the pita bread, if using.

WEIGHING BEANS
As a rough guide, you will need to buy about 1 pound 10 ounces fava beans in their pods to get about 2⅓ cups when shelled.

PER SERVING: 446 CALS | 13.7G FAT | 2.5G SAT FAT | 67.7G CARBS | 8.4G SUGARS | 15.5G FIBER | 19.1G PROTEIN | 920MG SODIUM

ROOT VEGETABLE CHIPS WITH HERBED YOGURT DIP

Making your own vegetables chips is surprisingly easy, and you can be sure there won't be any added artificial flavorings or preservatives.

SERVES: 4

PREP: 30 MINS   COOK: 16 MINS   COOL: 15 MINS

2¼ pounds mixed root vegetables, such as carrots, parsnips or sweet potatoes, and golden beets, thinly sliced
¼ cup virgin olive oil
sea salt and pepper (optional)

HERBED GARLIC DIP
1 cup Greek-style plain yogurt
2 garlic cloves, finely chopped
¼ cup finely chopped fresh herbs, such as flat-leaf parsley, chives, basil, and oregano

1. Preheat the oven to 400°F. To make the herbed garlic dip, spoon the yogurt into a small bowl, then stir in the garlic and herbs and season with salt and pepper, if using. Cover and chill in the refrigerator.

2. Put the vegetables in a large bowl. Slowly drizzle with the oil, gently turning the vegetables as you work, until they are all coated.

3. Arrange the vegetables over three baking sheets in a single layer, then season with salt and pepper, if using. Bake for 8–10 minutes, then check—the slices in the corners of the baking sheets will cook more quickly, so transfer any that are crisp and golden to a wire rack. Cook the rest for an additional 2–3 minutes, then transfer any additional cooked chips to the wire rack. Cook the remaining slices for another 2–3 minutes, if needed, then transfer to the wire rack and let cool.

4. Arrange the vegetable chips in a bowl and spoon the dip into a smaller bowl, then serve.

SLICING ROOTS
When thinly slicing root vegetables, you should ideally use a mandoline slicer. If you don't have one, a sharp small knife will do the job.

PER SERVING: 320 CALS | 16.4G FAT | 3.7G SAT FAT | 37.7G CARBS | 14.7G SUGARS | 8.4G FIBER | 7.8G PROTEIN | 720MG SODIUM

TURKEY NUGGETS WITH RED CABBAGE AND KALE SLAW

Forget deep-fried chicken; this oven-baked, crispy-coated turkey version is quick and easy to make, and healthier.

SERVES: 4
PREP: 20 MINS   COOK: 15 MINS

⅓ cup flaxseed
⅓ cup sesame seeds
2 eggs
1 pound skinless, boneless turkey breast, thinly sliced
3 tablespoons virgin olive oil
sea salt and pepper (optional)

RED CABBAGE AND KALE SLAW

1¼ cups thinly shredded red cabbage
⅓ cup thinly shredded kale
1 carrot, shredded
1 Golden Delicious, Red Delicious, Pink Lady, or other sweet, crisp apple, cored and coarsely grated
1 teaspoon caraway seeds
¼ cup Greek–style plain yogurt

1. Preheat the oven to 425°F and put a large baking sheet in it to preheat.

2. To make the slaw, put the red cabbage, kale, and carrot in a bowl and mix well. Add the apple, caraway seeds, and yogurt, season with salt and pepper, if using, and mix well. Cover and chill in the refrigerator until needed.

3. Put the flaxseed in a spice mill or blender and process until coarsely ground. Add the sesame seeds and process for a few seconds. Turn out the mixture onto a plate.

4. Crack the eggs into a shallow dish, season with salt and pepper, if using, and beat lightly with a fork.

5. Dip each turkey slice into the eggs, then lift it out with a fork and dip both sides into the seed mixture to coat. Brush the hot baking sheet with a little oil, add the turkey slices in a single layer, then drizzle with a little extra oil.

6. Bake the turkey, turning the slices once and moving them from the corners into the center of the baking sheet, for 15 minutes, or until golden brown and cooked through. Cut one of the larger turkey nuggets in half to check that the meat is no longer pink. Any juices that run out should be clear and piping hot with steam rising. Serve the nuggets with the slaw.

MAKE IT LIGHTER
Put a little oil in a small pump–action plastic sprayer and use it to spray a fine oil mist over the turkey before baking.

PER SERVING: 471 CALS | 27G FAT | 4.2G SAT FAT | 21.3G CARBS | 8.6G SUGARS | 9.2G FIBER | 38.4G PROTEIN | 720MG SODIUM

TAGLIATELLE WITH ROASTED SQUASH AND WALNUT PESTO

Roasted butternut squash or pumpkin tastes great with homemade walnut pesto. Make extra pesto and keep it in the refrigerator for up to two days.

SERVES: 4
PREP: 20 MINS   COOK: 25 MINS

3 cups seeded and peeled ³/₄-inch butternut squash or pumpkin slices
2 tablespoons virgin olive oil
1 pound fresh whole-wheat tagliatelle
sea salt flakes and pepper (optional)

WALNUT PESTO
³/₄ cup walnut pieces
¹/₃ cup virgin olive oil
¹/₃ cup fresh basil
1 ounce Parmesan cheese, thinly shaved, plus extra to serve
2¹/₂ cups arugula leaves

1. Preheat the oven to 400°F. Arrange the squash on a large baking sheet in a single layer. Drizzle with the oil and season with salt and pepper, if using. Roast for 20–25 minutes, or until just tender.

2. Meanwhile, to make the pesto, put the walnuts in a large skillet and toast for 2–3 minutes, or until just beginning to brown. Transfer to a food processor or blender, pour in the oil, and process until coarsely ground. Add the basil, cheese, and half the arugula leaves and process again until you have a coarse pesto.

3. Bring a large saucepan of water to a boil, add the tagliatelle, and cook for 3–4 minutes, or according to the package directions, until tender but still firm to the bite.

4. Drain the pasta, reserving a little of the cooking water. Return the pasta to the pan. Cut the squash into cubes and add them to the pasta. Drizzle with the pesto and gently toss together, adding a little of the reserved pasta water if needed to loosen the sauce. Top with the remaining arugula.

5. Spoon into bowls and serve with extra cheese.

MAKE IT LIGHTER
Toss the roasted squash and walnut pesto with crisp salad greens instead of pasta for a lighter meal.

PER SERVING: 808 CALS | 49.9G FAT | 8.2G SAT FAT | 74.7G CARBS | 4.5G SUGARS | 11.1G FIBER | 25.5G PROTEIN | 760MG SODIUM

ROASTED BEET AND FARRO SALAD

Beets are low in fat, full of vitamins and minerals, packed with antioxidants, and delicious, especially when sharing a plate with earthy farro and walnuts.

SERVES: 4
PREP: 20 MINS   COOK: 40 MINS

2 raw beets, quartered
3 sprigs of fresh thyme
⅓ cup walnut oil
⅔ cup farro, rinsed
½ teaspoon salt
1 large red bell pepper, halved lengthwise and seeded
¼ cup coarsely chopped walnuts
3 cups arugula leaves
thick balsamic vinegar, for drizzling
sea salt and pepper (optional)

1. Preheat the oven to 375°F. Preheat the broiler to high. Cut out two squares of aluminum foil.

2. Divide the beets and thyme between the foil squares. Sprinkle with a little of the oil and season with salt and pepper, if using. Wrap in a loose package, sealing the edges, and place on a baking sheet. Roast for 30–40 minutes, or until tender.

3. Meanwhile, put the farro in a saucepan, cover with water, and add ½ teaspoon of salt. Bring to a boil, then reduce the heat, cover, and simmer for 20 minutes, or according to the package directions, until the grains are tender. Drain the farro and transfer to a dish.

4. Meanwhile, put the red bell pepper halves, cut side down, on the broiler pan and broil for 10 minutes, or until blackened. Cover with a clean dish towel and let stand for 10 minutes. Remove and discard the skin and coarsely chop the flesh.

5. Divide the cooked farro among four plates. Slice the beet quarters in half, arrange on top of the farro, and toss. Sprinkle with the red pepper, walnuts, and arugula.

6. Drizzle with the remaining oil and some balsamic vinegar. Serve immediately.

ALSO TRY
This salad works equally well with barley instead of farro. The barley will need boiling for 35 minutes.

PER SERVING: 315 CALS | 21.9G FAT | 2G SAT FAT | 25.6G CARBS | 7.6G SUGARS | 4.3G FIBER | 5.8G PROTEIN | 640MG SODIUM

SPICY HAMBURGERS WITH GUACAMOLE AND WEDGES

A good hamburger is hard to beat, and if you make your own, you'll know what is in it and where the meat has come from. Grind the steak in a food processor or meat grinder.

SERVES: 4
PREP: 35 MINS, PLUS CHILLING RISE: 1½ HOURS
COOK: 45 MINUTES

1 pound sirloin steak, visible fat removed, diced
½ teaspoon chili powder
2 teaspoons cumin seeds, coarsely crushed
1 tablespoon fresh thyme leaves
5 russet potatoes, unpeeled, scrubbed, and cut into wedges
3 tablespoons virgin olive oil
1 teaspoon paprika
sea salt and pepper (optional)

GUACAMOLE
1 large avocado, pitted and peeled
juice of 1 lime
2 scallions, finely chopped

TO SERVE
4 spelt rolls, halved
1 romaine lettuce heart, shredded
handful of arugula leaves
2 large tomatoes, sliced

1. Preheat the oven to 400° F. With the motor running on a food processor, drop in a few pieces of steak at a time, until it has all been coarsely chopped. Alternatively, press the pieces through a manual meat grinder on the coarse setting.

2. Put the chili powder, half the cumin seeds, half the thyme, and a little salt and pepper, if using, into a bowl and mix well. Rub it into the steak, then shape the mixture into four patties. Cover and chill in the refrigerator for 15 minutes.

3. Meanwhile, bring a saucepan of water to a boil, add the potato wedges, and cook for 4–5 minutes, or until almost tender. Drain well and transfer to a roasting pan. Drizzle the wedges with 2 tablespoons of oil, then turn them several times until they are well coated. Sprinkle with the paprika, remaining cumin and thyme, and a little salt and pepper, if using. Bake, turning once, for 25–30 minutes, or until golden brown.

4. For the guacamole, put the avocado in a shallow bowl and mash with a fork. Add the lime juice and scallions, season with a little salt and pepper, if using, and mix well.

5. Preheat the broiler to medium–high. Brush the patties with a little of the remaining oil, then cook, turning halfway through, for 8–10 minutes, or a little less for those who prefer their burgers pink in the middle. Let stand for a few minutes. Meanwhile, toast the rolls, then top the bottom half of the rolls with lettuce, arugula, and tomatoes, the hot burgers, and a spoonful of guacamole before finishing with the lids. Serve with the potato wedges.

AVOCADO TIP
Avocado flesh quickly turns brown, so don't peel and mash the flesh for the guacamole until you are ready to cook the burgers.

PER SERVING: 695 CALS | 28.9G FAT | 5.8G SAT FAT | 63.4G CARBS | 9.9G SUGARS | 13.8G FIBER | 49.1G PROTEIN | 560MG SODIUM

SPICED TURKEY STEW WITH WHOLE-GRAIN COUSCOUS

*Capture the flavors of Middle Eastern cooking with this easy,
lightly spiced stove-top turkey stew.*

SERVES: 4
PREP: 20 MINS   COOK: 25 MINS

1 tablespoon virgin olive oil
1 pound skinless, boneless turkey
breast, cut into ¾-inch pieces
1 onion, coarsely chopped
2 garlic cloves, finely chopped
1 red and 1 orange bell pepper, seeded
and coarsely chopped
4 tomatoes, coarsely chopped
1 teaspoon cumin seeds, coarsely crushed
1 teaspoon paprika
finely grated zest and juice of 1 unwaxed lemon
sea salt and pepper (optional)

TO SERVE

1 cup whole-grain giant couscous
2 tablespoons coarsely chopped fresh flat-leaf parsley
2 tablespoons coarsely chopped fresh cilantro

1. Heat the oil in a large skillet over medium heat. Add the turkey, a few pieces at a time, then add the onion. Sauté, stirring, for 5 minutes, or until the turkey is golden.

2. Add the garlic, red and orange bell peppers, and tomatoes, then stir in the cumin seeds and paprika. Add the lemon juice and season with salt and pepper, if using. Stir well, then cover and cook, stirring from time to time, for 20 minutes, or until the tomatoes have formed a thick sauce and the turkey is cooked through and the juices run clear with no sign of pink when a piece is cut in half.

3. Meanwhile, fill a saucepan halfway with water and bring to a boil. Add the couscous and cook according to the package directions, or until just tender. Transfer to a strainer and drain well.

4. Spoon the couscous onto plates and top with the turkey stew. Mix the parsley and cilantro with the lemon zest, then sprinkle the mixture over the stew and serve.

GOOD TURKEY
Turkey makes a great low-fat, quick-cook
dinner, especially without the skin.

PER SERVING: 399 CALS | 6.6G FAT | 1.3G SAT FAT | 36G CARBS | 8.1G SUGARS | 7.2G FIBER | 37.5G PROTEIN | 360MG SODIUM

CHICKEN WITH POMEGRANATE AND BEET TABBOULEH

*This version of tabbouleh is made with whole-grain wheat berries.
High in fiber, it is a great alternative to rice or pasta.*

SERVES: 4
PREP: 25 MINS   COOK: 25 MINS

1⅓ cups wheat berries
4 raw beets, cut into cubes
1 pound skinless, boneless chicken
breasts, thinly sliced
1 small red onion, thinly sliced
12 cherry tomatoes, halved
seeds of 1 small pomegranate
2 tablespoons coarsely chopped fresh mint
2½ cups baby spinach

DRESSING
juice of 1 lemon
¼ cup virgin olive oil
2 garlic cloves, finely chopped
1 teaspoon packed light brown sugar
sea salt and pepper (optional)

1. Fill the bottom of a steamer with water, bring to a boil, then add the wheat berries to the water. Put the beets in the steamer top, cover with a lid, and steam for 20–25 minutes, or until the wheat berries and beets are cooked. Drain the wheat berries.

2. Meanwhile, to make the dressing, put the lemon juice, oil, garlic, and sugar in a screw-lid jar, season with salt and pepper, if using, then screw on the lid and shake well.

3. Put the chicken in a bowl, add half the dressing, and toss well. Preheat a ridged grill pan over medium-high heat. Add the chicken and cook, turning once or twice, for 8–10 minutes, or until golden and cooked through. Cut one of the larger slices of chicken in half to check that the meat is no longer pink. Any juices that run out should be clear and piping hot with steam rising.

4. Put the red onion, tomatoes, and pomegranate seeds in a large shallow bowl. Add the wheat berries, beets, and mint. Divide the spinach among four plates, spoon the wheat berry mixture over them, then arrange the chicken on top. Serve with the remaining dressing in a small pitcher.

LOVE LEFTOVERS
Leftovers can be packed in plastic containers and stored in the refrigerator—but keep the dressing separate so that the salad doesn't go limp.

PER SERVING: 545 CALS | 17.2G FAT | 2G SAT FAT | 62.2G CARBS | 15G SUGARS | 12.3G FIBER | 39.4G PROTEIN | 440MG SODIUM

BUTTER-FRIED SOLE

*Look for sustainable fish caught the day you plan to eat it—
the flavor will be much better. Frozen fish is also recommended,
because it's often caught and frozen on the same day.*

SERVES: 2
PREP: 20 MINS   COOK: 12 MINS

½ cup milk
⅓ cup brown rice flour
4 sole fillets, 6 ounces each, skinned
16 asparagus spears
6 tablespoons unsalted butter
juice of ½ lemon, plus 1 lemon, cut into
wedges, to serve
sea salt and pepper (optional)
2 tablespoons coarsely chopped fresh flat-leaf
parsley, to garnish

1. Pour the milk into a shallow bowl at least as large as each fillet and put the flour on a plate. Season each fillet on both sides with salt and pepper, if using.

2. Bring a saucepan of water to a boil, add the asparagus, and cook for 3–5 minutes, then drain well and keep warm.

3. Working with one sole fillet at a time, pull it quickly through the milk, then dip it in the flour, turn once to coat all over, and shake off any excess flour. Transfer it to a plate and continue until all the fillets are prepared.

4. Melt half the butter in a skillet large enough to hold the fillets in a single layer over medium-high heat. Add the fillets, skinned side down, and cook for 2 minutes.

5. Turn over the fillets and cook for 2–3 minutes, or until the flesh flakes easily. Transfer to two plates, skinned side up, and set aside.

6. Reduce the heat to medium and melt the remaining butter in the pan. When it stops foaming, add the lemon juice and stir, scraping the sediment from the bottom of the pan. Spoon the butter mixture over the fish and garnish with parsley. Serve with the asparagus and lemon wedges.

BUYING ASPARAGUS
To check for freshness, bend the bottom
of the asparagus—you should be able
to bend only the end of it.

PER SERVING: 753 CALS | 44.1G FAT | 24.5G SAT FAT | 39G CARBS | 6.2G SUGARS | 7.7G FIBER | 52.7G PROTEIN | 2,000MG SODIUM

BAKED PARSNIPS AND TOMATOES

Serve this dish with fresh salad and whole-wheat bread as a tasty vegetable dinner, or as a side dish with roasted meat.

SERVES: 4
PREP: 30 MINS   COOK: 50 MINS

3 tablespoons virgin olive oil
5 parsnips, thinly sliced lengthwise
1 teaspoon fresh thyme leaves
1¼ cups heavy cream
5 tomatoes, thinly sliced
1 teaspoon dried oregano
1⅓ cups shredded cheddar cheese
sea salt and pepper (optional)

1. Preheat the oven to 350°F. Heat the oil in a skillet over medium heat. Add the parsnips and thyme and season with salt and pepper, if using. Cook, stirring often, for 6–8 minutes, or until softened. Do this in batches if necessary.

2. Spread half the parsnips over the bottom of a gratin dish. Pour over half the cream, then arrange half the tomatoes in an even layer on top. Season with salt and pepper, if using, and sprinkle over half the oregano and half the cheddar cheese. Top with the remaining parsnips and tomatoes. Sprinkle with the remaining oregano, season with salt and pepper, if using, and pour the remaining cream over the vegetables. Sprinkle with the last of the cheddar cheese.

3. Cover with aluminum foil and bake for 40 minutes, or until the parsnips are tender. Remove the foil and return to the oven for 5–10 minutes, or until the top is golden and bubbling. Serve immediately.

ALSO TRY
Use Parmesan cheese instead of cheddar, or mozzarella for a pizza-style stringy texture.

PER SERVING: 639 CALS | 51G FAT | 26.7G SAT FAT | 35.4G CARBS | 11.4G SUGARS | 9.1G FIBER | 13.9G PROTEIN | 560MG SODIUM

CELEBRATION CHOCOLATE CAKE

No one would guess from the appearance of this indulgent-looking cake that it is made with cooked beets for natural sweetness and whole-wheat and brown rice flours.

SERVES 8

PREP: 40 MINS   COOK: 1 HOUR 20 MINS   COOL: 15 MINS

2½ raw beets, cut into cubes
5½ ounces semisweet chocolate, broken into pieces
¼ cup unsweetened cocoa powder
2 teaspoons baking powder
1 cup whole-wheat flour
⅓ cup brown rice flour
1¾ sticks unsalted butter, softened and diced, plus extra to grease
1 cup plus 2 tablespoons firmly packed light brown sugar
4 eggs
2 tablespoons milk
1¼ cups heavy cream

1. Preheat the oven to 325°F. Lightly butter an 8-inch diameter round nonstick springform cake pan and line the bottom with a circle of parchment paper.

2. Fill the bottom of a steamer halfway with water, bring to a boil, then put the beets in the steamer top, cover with a lid, and steam for 15 minutes, or until tender. Transfer to a food processor and add ¼ cup of water from the bottom of the steamer. Puree until smooth, then let cool.

3. Put 4 ounces of the chocolate in a heatproof bowl set over a saucepan of gently simmering water, making sure the bowl doesn't touch the water. Let heat for 5 minutes, or until the chocolate has melted.

4. Sift the cocoa into a second bowl, then stir in the baking powder and whole-wheat and rice flours.

5. Cream the butter and 1 cup of the sugar together in a large bowl. Beat in the eggs, one by one, adding spoonfuls of the flour mixture between each egg and beating well after each addition. Stir in the remaining flour mixture, the pureed beet, and melted chocolate, and beat until smooth, then mix in enough of the milk to make a soft dropping consistency.

6. Spoon the batter into the prepared pan and spread it into an even layer. Bake for 1 hour, or until well risen, the top is slightly cracked, and a toothpick comes out cleanly when inserted into the center of the cake. Let cool for 15 minutes, then remove from the pan, peel off the parchment paper, and transfer the cake to a wire rack.

7. To finish, melt the remaining chocolate in a heatproof bowl set over a saucepan of gently simmering water, making sure the bowl doesn't touch the water. Put the cream in a separate bowl, add the remaining 2 tablespoons of sugar, and beat until soft swirls form. Cut the cake in half and put the bottom half on a serving plate. Spoon one-third of the cream mixture onto the bottom of the cake, add the top half of the cake, then spoon the remaining cream on top. Drizzle with the melted chocolate. Cut into eight wedges to serve.

DARK CHOCOLATE
Studies show that eating a little dark chocolate every day can help lower your blood pressure.

PER SERVING: 662 CALS | 46.2G FAT | 27.5G SAT FAT | 57G CARBS | 33.7G SUGARS | 5.7G FIBER | 9.5G PROTEIN | 400MG SODIUM

APPLESAUCE SPICED CUPCAKES

*These lemony apple cupcakes are satisfying and wholesome,
containing brown sugar and whole-wheat flour.*

MAKES: 12 CUPCAKES
PREP: 40 MINS   COOK: 1 HOUR 15 MINS   COOL: 30 MINS

3 Rome, Pippin, or other sweet, crisp apples
finely grated zest and juice of 1 unwaxed lemon
2/3 cup whole-wheat flour
1/2 cup brown rice flour
2 teaspoons baking powder
1/2 teaspoon ground allspice, plus extra to decorate
1 stick unsalted butter, softened and diced
1/2 cup firmly packed light brown sugar
2 eggs, beaten
1 cup crème fraîche or plain Greek-style yogurt

1. To make the applesauce, peel, core, and coarsely chop two of the apples, then put them in a saucepan. Add the lemon zest and half the juice, cover, and cook over medium-low heat for 5–10 minutes, or until soft. Mash until smooth, then let cool. Preheat the oven to 350°F.

2. Put 12 paper liners or squares of parchment paper in a 12-section muffin pan. Put the whole-wheat and rice flours, baking powder, and allspice into a bowl and mix well.

3. Cream the butter and sugar together in a large bowl. Beat in alternate spoonfuls of the eggs and the flour mixture until it is all used, then stir in 2/3 cup applesauce (reserve any remaining for another time).

4. Spoon the batter into the paper liners. Bake for 15–18 minutes, or until well risen and the tops spring back when pressed with a fingertip. Let cool for 5 minutes, then transfer to a wire rack.

5. Line a baking sheet with parchment paper. Put the rest of the lemon juice in a medium bowl. Thinly slice the remaining apple, toss it in the lemon juice, then arrange it on the prepared baking sheet. Reduce the oven temperature to 225°F and cook the apple slices, turning once, for 30–45 minutes, or until just beginning to brown. Turn off the oven and let the apples cool inside it. Lift off the slices with a spatula and cut them in half.

6. Top each cupcake with a spoonful of crème fraîche or yogurt, sprinkle with allspice, and put two apple slices on top.

MAKE IT SIMPLE
These cakes are great without any decoration, and make a healthy addition to the kids' school lunch bags.

PER CAKE: 224 CALS | 12.8G FAT | 7.5G SAT FAT | 25.6G CARBS | 13.9G SUGARS | 1.9G FIBER | 3.2G PROTEIN | 240MG SODIUM

RASPBERRY RICOTTA CHEESECAKE

Traditionally, cheesecakes have a crushed cookie crust, but this granola-style crust is packed with protein-filled nuts and cholesterol-lowering oats.

SERVES: 8

PREP: 40 MINS   COOK: 15 MINS

SOAK: 5 MINS   CHILL: 6 HOURS

2 tablespoons unsalted butter
1 tablespoon virgin olive oil, plus extra to grease
1/3 cup maple syrup, plus extra to serve
1/2 cup rolled oats
1/2 cup coarsely chopped unblanched almonds
1/2 cup coarsely chopped unblanched hazelnuts

TOPPING

1/4 cup cold water
2 1/2 teaspoons gelatin powder
1 cup ricotta cheese
1 cup mascarpone cheese
1 cup plain yogurt
finely grated zest and juice of 1 unwaxed lemon, plus extra zest to decorate
1 1/4 cups raspberries

1. To make the crust, preheat the oven to 325°F. Brush a 9-inch-diameter round nonstick springform tart pan with a little oil. Put the butter, oil, and 2 tablespoons of maple syrup in a saucepan over medium-low heat until the butter has melted. Remove the pan from the heat and stir in the oats and nuts.

2. Transfer the mixture into the prepared pan and press down into an even layer with the back of a fork. Bake for 15 minutes, or until golden, then let cool.

3. To make the topping, spoon the water into a small heatproof bowl, then sprinkle the gelatin over the top, making sure all the powder is absorbed. Soak for 5 minutes. Place the bowl over a saucepan of gently simmering water until you have a clear liquid.

4. Put the ricotta, mascarpone, and yogurt in a bowl, spoon in the remaining 1/4 cup of maple syrup, and beat until smooth. Mix in the lemon zest and juice, then gradually beat in the gelatin mixture. Add half the raspberries and crush them into the mixture with a fork.

5. Spoon the topping onto the crust and smooth the surface, then sprinkle with the remaining raspberries. Cover the cheesecake and chill in the refrigerator for 4–6 hours, or until set.

6. To serve, run a knife around the edge of the pan, release the side, and slide the cheesecake onto a serving plate. Decorate with the remaining lemon zest. To serve, cut into wedges and drizzle with extra maple syrup.

FREEZE IT

This cheesecake can be frozen for up to two months. Wrap the pan in plastic wrap, seal, and label. Defrost in the refrigerator for four hours, then for one hour at room temperature.

PER SERVING: 389 CALS | 29.3G FAT | 14.3G SAT FAT | 22.9G CARBS | 14.1G SUGARS | 3.2G FIBER | 11G PROTEIN | 80MG SODIUM

MANGO FRUITY CRUSH ICE POPS

These three-layered fruity, creamy treats are packed with color, texture, and flavor. The mango and strawberries work hand in hand with the vanilla.

MAKES: 8 ICE POPS
PREP: 20 MINS   FREEZE: 8 HOURS

1 mango, peeled, pitted, and cubed
½ cup plus 1 tablespoon honey
1¼ cups plain yogurt
2 teaspoons vanilla extract
2 cups hulled strawberry pieces

YOU WILL ALSO NEED:
8 (½-cup) ice pop molds
8 ice pop sticks

1. Put the mango in a blender or food processor and process to a puree. Transfer to a small bowl, add 3 tablespoons of honey, and stir well.

2. Pour the mixture into eight ½-cup ice pop molds. Freeze for 2 hours, or until firm.

3. When the mango mixture is frozen, put the yogurt, vanilla extract, and 3 tablespoons of honey in a bowl and stir well. Spoon it over the frozen mango mixture. Insert the ice pop sticks, and freeze for 2–3 hours, or until firm.

4. When the vanilla mixture is frozen, put the strawberries and remaining 3 tablespoons of honey in a blender and process to a puree. Strain out the seeds with a fine metal strainer. Pour it over the frozen vanilla mixture and freeze for 2–3 hours, or until firm.

5. To unmold the ice pops, dip the frozen molds into warm water for a few seconds and gently release the ice pops while holding the sticks.

MMM, MANGO
Mangoes contain a selection of vitamins and minerals, and are particularly rich in vitamin C and beta-carotene, which the body converts into vitamin A.

PER ICE POP: 141 CALS | 0.7G FAT | 0.3G SAT FAT | 33.3G CARBS | 31.7G SUGARS | 1.4G FIBER | 2.5G PROTEIN | TRACE SODIUM

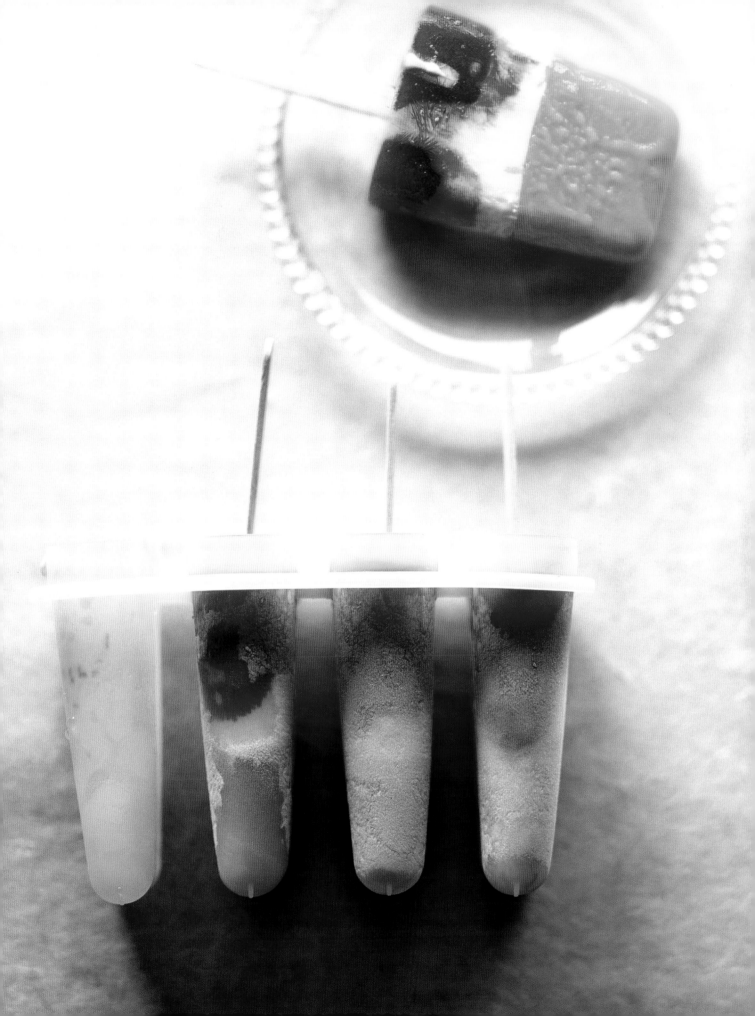

PROTEIN

WHAT IS PROTEIN?

Protein is one of the major nutrients our bodies need for health, growth, and normal functioning, and we need to consume it regularly. It is a component of many foods, but it doesn't always take the same form. It consists of combinations of amino acids—often called protein's "building blocks"—that are vital for every metabolic process in our bodies and make up a large proportion of our cells, muscles, and tissue. Protein-containing foods vary in the amount and type of these amino acids that they contain.

Protein is essential for building, maintaining, and repairing cells and for the actual structure of cells. It also helps protect us from viral and bacterial infections and boosts the immune system; acts as a coordinator between various body processes; helps with body movement; and transports atoms and molecules around the body. Surplus protein can also be converted into energy (calories).

Our total protein needs may alter according to our circumstances. Body weight is perhaps the most important factor—sedentary adults need about 0.5 gram of protein a day per pound of their weight. Pregnant and breast-feeding women need more protein than average, while factors such as age and activity levels alter our optimum intake.

Most adults in the United States and other Western countries do eat enough protein, according to official figures, but protein deficiency and malnutrition throughout the world is common. High activity levels increase protein needs by up to 50 percent and some research shows that older people may need about 25 percent more protein than younger adults. While vegetarians don't need more protein than anyone else, they need to get a good daily variety of protein-containing foods to get all the essential amino acids.

The recipes in this chapter include a balanced mix of natural protein types including vegetable, meat, fish, and dairy proteins. The vegetable-base recipes aren't necessarily strictly vegetarian or vegan, so check the ingredients list.

Your protein intake can be improved by making good choices at any meal of the day. Healthy breakfasts, lunches, snacks, dinners, and desserts that are higher in protein than perhaps your usual choices can help to increase your protein levels.

VEGETABLE-BASE PROTEINS

Vegetable-base protein sources are an excellent choice and offer a range of health and nutritional benefits. When people think of "protein" foods, they often think of animal sources, such as meat and fish. However, it is not difficult to get your daily requirements of protein by choosing more—or even all—from the wide range of vegetable-base foods. These include legumes, such as fresh and dried beans, peas, and lentils; nuts; and seeds. Many other types of vegetables are good or useful sources of protein.

Humans need 20 different types of amino acids. The body can manufacture 11 of these, but the other 9 are called essential (or indispensible) because they must come from the diet. Individual foods that do contain all of the essential amino acids are called "complete proteins."

Few individual vegetable-base protein foods are classified as "complete proteins," but all vegetable sources do contain a mix of some or most of the essential amino acids. If you eat a good variety of vegetable protein sources every day, then you should get enough. Soybeans, quinoa, amaranth, buckwheat, and chia seeds contain all 9 essential amino acids and are, therefore, classified as complete proteins.

LEGUMES

Dried beans, peas, and lentils are a major source of protein in a vegetable-base diet, because they can be eaten in place of animal protein sources and lower-protein carbs, such as rice and potatoes. They are also rich in various vitamins and minerals as well as fiber and plant chemicals.

NUTS AND SEEDS

Although we tend to eat nuts and seeds in smaller quantity, they are a valuable protein source as well as containing important unsaturated fats and a variety of vitamins and minerals, fiber, and plant chemicals.

GRAINS AND PSEUDO GRAINS

Rolled oats and whole wheat are popular and traditionally thought of as carb foods, but they are surprisingly high in protein. Other grains, such as spelt, wild rice, quinoa (not actually a grain but a seed), and amaranth contain especially useful amounts of protein.

VEGETABLES

All plant foods contain at least some protein, and several vegetables supply good amounts, including leafy greens, such as spinach, cabbage, and broccoli, fresh peas, and beans.

EGGS AND DAIRY-BASE PROTEINS

Milk, cheese, and yogurt are an important part of a protein-rich diet for many vegetarians, and they are also a great source of calcium, while eggs contain a range of vitamins and minerals.

EGGS

Several research studies on eggs show that a breakfast or meal containing eggs can help reduce hunger throughout the day and limit calorie intake. They are a good source of the B vitamins as well as iron, zinc, and selenium.

Egg whites are cholesterol free, low-calorie, and 85 percent protein. An average egg contains only one-third of its fat as saturates, while over one-third are healthy monounsaturates.

If you buy organic eggs from hens allowed unlimited access to organic pastures and woodland, they will naturally have a higher content of omega-3 fats, the healthy unsaturated group also found (in another form) in oily fish, a lower saturates level, and more vitamin E.

MILK AND YOGURT

Milk and yogurt can make a useful contribution to your daily protein intake. Not all milk and yogurt is high in saturated fat as is often thought. For example, regular Greek yogurt contains a higher level of protein than other types of yogurt and its saturated fat content is relatively low.

Milk and yogurt are good sources of calcium for healthy bones as well as the B vitamins. Whole milk is also a good source of vitamin A—low-fat versions are not, because the vitamin is found only in the fat.

Sheep and goat milk and yogurt are becoming more popular and more available.

CHEESE

Cheese is often thought of as one of the best sources of protein but some types have a much higher content than others.

Hard cheeses, such as cheddar, Parmesan, and Gruyère, are some of the best, while creamy and soft cheeses are often low in protein—the exceptions being soft goat cheese, ricotta, and quark.

Hard cheeses are a good source of calcium and the B vitamins, while regular (not reduced-fat) cheeses are a good source of vitamin A.

Organic milk, yogurt, and cheese tend to contain a better ratio of healthy unsaturated fats to saturated fats.

Meals and snacks containing cheese help to increase satiety and keep hunger at bay for longer.

MEAT AND FISH PROTEINS

Red and white meats, poultry, and fish have been recommended for decades as the best source of top-quality "complete protein." But in recent years there has been much conflicting evidence and advice about how much of them we should eat.

WHAT DOES TOP-QUALITY PROTEIN MEAN?

Top-quality protein means a protein source that contains all the essential amino acids in good proportions and that are easily absorbed by the digestive system.

Animal sources of protein, such as lean meat and fish, are excellent sources of top-quality complete proteins that are also well absorbed by most people.

DO WE NEED MEAT AND FISH?

No—vegetarian and vegan diets can, with care, provide the full range of nutrients. However, vegetables and meat/fish contain different nutrients needed for health (for example, red meat is high in easily absorbed iron and zinc while legumes contain less; legumes are rich in fiber while meats contain none; oily fish is a great source of omega-3 fat while vegetables contain little), so a diet that combines both could be an easy way to be sure you get all the nutrients you need.

But we shouldn't eat too much red meat (beef, lamb, pork, veal, venison, or goat). Check government guidelines for the latest advice.

The best idea is to use meat as a small component of a meal instead of "the main event." Because ounce for ounce, meat is higher in protein than most other protein sources, you can eat less and still meet your protein needs.

Chicken (and other poultry) doesn't fall under official advice on limitation. Choose lean chicken and avoid the fatty skin. Turkey breast is an especially low-fat and high-protein choice.

All fish and seafoods are a complete protein source and contain a range of vitamins and minerals. Check government guidelines for the latest advice on portion sizes.

OATMEAL WITH HOT SMOKED SALMON

You may think oatmeal is just for a sweet breakfast, but oats taste great combined with savory flavors and provide sustained energy throughout the morning. Adding salmon provides a protein and omega-3 boost.

SERVES: 4
PREP: 10 MINS   COOK: 12–15 MINS

1²/₃ cups rolled oats
1¹/₂ cups milk
2¹/₂ cups water
4 eggs
4 teaspoons creamed horseradish
7 ounces hot smoked salmon, flaked
2 avocados, pitted, peeled, and sliced
black pepper (optional)
2 tablespoons pumpkin seeds, toasted, to garnish

1. Put the oats into a saucepan with the milk and water. Bring to a boil and simmer for 4–5 minutes, until thick and creamy.

2. Meanwhile, poach the eggs in a saucepan of simmering water for 4–5 minutes.

3. Stir the creamed horseradish and half the smoked salmon into the oatmeal.

4. Divide the oatmeal among four warm bowls and top each one with slices of avocado, a poached egg, and the remaining salmon.

5. Serve the oatmeal sprinkled with toasted pumpkin seeds and seasoned with pepper, if using.

SOMETHING DIFFERENT
Sautéed mushrooms topped with a fried egg and a sprinkling of chives make a delicious variation.

PER SERVING: 547 CALS | 32.8G FAT | 7.1G SAT FAT | 37.9G CARBS | 6G SUGARS | 9.1G FIBER | 27.7G PROTEIN | 520MG SODIUM

ORANGE AND BANANA PANCAKES

Teff flour is milled from a fine grain grown mainly in Ethiopia, and it is known for its health-boosting and gluten-free properties. It has a subtle nutty flavor and complements pancakes wonderfully.

SERVES: 4
PREP: 5–10 MINS   COOK: 25 MINS

1 cup teff flour
½ teaspoon ground cinnamon
1 teaspoon baking powder
1 egg
¾ cup milk
2 tablespoons unsalted butter, melted
1 banana, peeled and diced
1 tablespoon melted coconut oil

TO SERVE
2 oranges, peeled and divided into sections
1 tablespoon sesame seeds, toasted
maple syrup (optional)

1. Mix the flour, cinnamon, and baking powder together in a large bowl.

2. Whisk the egg and milk together in a separate bowl, then whisk into the flour mixture until smooth; the batter should be the consistency of thick, heavy cream. Add a little more milk, if needed.

3. Stir the melted butter and banana into the pancake batter.

4. Heat the coconut oil in a skillet over medium heat, then spoon in tablespoons of the batter. Cook for 3–4 minutes, until the pancakes are golden underneath, then flip over and cook for an additional 2–3 minutes.

5. Repeat with the remaining batter until you have 12 pancakes.

6. Serve the pancakes topped with the orange sections, a sprinkling of toasted sesame seeds, and a drizzle of maple syrup, if using.

WHY NOT TRY?
These pancakes can be served with other fresh fruits, honey, or a dollop of plain yogurt.

PER SERVING: 315 CALS | 14.1G FAT | 8.2G SAT FAT | 40.2G CARBS | 12.5G SUGARS | 5.1G FIBER | 9G PROTEIN | 160MG SODIUM

QUINOA AND CASHEW NUT PORRIDGE

*Creamy and delicious porridge doesn't have to be made with oats.
Quinoa provides much more protein and doesn't contain any wheat.
Cashew nuts also add essential minerals, including magnesium and potassium.*

SERVES: 4
PREP: 5–10 MINS   COOK: 12–15 MINS

1 cup quinoa
1/4 cup coarsely chopped cashew nuts
4 1/4 cups almond milk
1 vanilla bean, halved and seeds removed
1 apple, grated
1 teaspoon ground cinnamon
1 tablespoon maple syrup
2 tablespoons chia seeds

TO SERVE
3/4 cup raspberries
1/3 cup blueberries
2 tablespoons pomegranate seeds

1. Put the quinoa into a saucepan with the nuts, milk, vanilla seeds, apple, cinnamon, and maple syrup. Bring to a boil, then simmer for 10–12 minutes.

2. Stir the chia seeds into the pan and stir well.

3. Spoon the porridge into four bowls and serve topped with the raspberries, blueberries, and pomegranate seeds.

MIX IT UP
Serve this porridge with the fruit and nuts of your choice. Try to use fruits that are in season, such as berries in the summer, and apples and pears through the cooler months.

PER SERVING: 332 CALS | 11G FAT | 1.1G SAT FAT | 49.9G CARBS | 10.7G SUGARS | 9G FIBER | 13.4G PROTEIN | 160MG SODIUM

SPINACH AND NUTMEG BAKED EGGS

Nutrient-rich fresh spinach adds delicious flavor and color to this popular egg dish, lightly seasoned with ground nutmeg. Serve with standard or gluten-free bread for a wholesome breakfast or brunch.

SERVES: 4

PREP: 20 MINS   COOK: 20–30 MINS

1 tablespoon olive oil, for brushing
1 tablespoon olive oil, for frying
4 shallots, finely chopped
3 garlic cloves, sliced
3½ cups baby spinach
8 eggs
½ teaspoon ground nutmeg
salt and pepper (optional)

1. Preheat the oven to 350°F. Lightly brush the insides of four 1-cup ramekins (individual ceramic dishes) with olive oil.

2. Heat the olive oil in a skillet. When hot, add the shallots and garlic and sauté over medium heat for 3–4 minutes, or until soft. Add the baby spinach and stir for 2–3 minutes, or until just wilted. Season with salt and pepper, if using.

3. Spoon the spinach mixture into the bottom of the prepared ramekins and crack two eggs into each. Sprinkle with the nutmeg and place the ramekins in a roasting pan. Fill the roasting pan with boiling water until the water reaches halfway up the ramekins—this creates a steamy environment for the eggs so there is no chance of them drying out.

4. Carefully transfer the roasting pan to the preheated oven for 15–20 minutes. Let the ramekins cool slightly, then serve immediately.

SUPER SPINACH

Researchers have found many flavonoid compounds in spinach act as antioxidants and fight against stomach, skin, breast, prostate, and other cancers.

PER SERVING: 235 CALS | 16.5G FAT | 4.2G SAT FAT | 7.5G CARBS | 1.6G SUGARS | 1.1G FIBER | 14.2G PROTEIN | 160MG SODIUM

BERRY POWER SMOOTHIE

Breakfast is arguably the most important meal of the day, and this shake includes loads of vital nutrients. It's quick to make, tasty, and filling, but it won't leave you feeling heavy.

SERVES: 1
PREP: 15 MINS   COOK: NONE

2 tablespoons pumpkin seeds
2 tablespoons flaxseed
3 tablespoons slivered almonds
1 cup raspberries
¾ cup blueberries
1 cup vanilla soy yogurt
½ cup chilled water

1. Put the pumpkin seeds, flaxseed, and almonds into a blender and blend until finely ground.

2. Add the raspberries, blueberries, yogurt, and chilled water and blend until smooth.

3. Pour into a glass and serve.

POWERFUL PUMPKIN SEEDS

These little seeds are really nutritious and, even in small servings, they provide a significant amount of minerals, especially zinc and iron.

PER SERVING: 641 CALS | 33.8G FAT | 3.7G SAT FAT | 72.7G CARBS | 41.8G SUGARS | 19.9G FIBER | 22.1G PROTEIN | 40MG SODIUM

POKE BOWL

A poke bowl is a staple Hawaiian dish that normally contains raw fish and plenty of vibrant ingredients, both hot and cold. This recipe includes tuna for protein and wakame for magnesium, iodine, and calcium.

SERVES: 4
PREP: 15 MINS, PLUS SOAKING   COOK: 25 MINS

1 cup brown rice
³/₄ cup wakame, soaked in lukewarm water for
10–15 minutes and coarsely chopped
2 tablespoons soy sauce
2 tablespoons rice wine vinegar
8 ounces good-quality raw tuna, sliced
1 avocado, pitted, peeled, and sliced
8 cherry tomatoes, halved
4 scallions, thinly sliced
½ teaspoon crushed red pepper flakes
2 tablespoons olive oil
1 tablespoon black sesame seeds

1. Cook the rice according to the package directions.

2. Put the cooked rice into a bowl and stir in half the soaked wakame, half the soy sauce, and the rice wine vinegar. Divide among four bowls and top with the tuna, avocado, tomatoes, and scallions.

3. Mix the remaining soy sauce and wakame with the crushed red pepper flakes, olive oil, and sesame seeds in a small bowl. Sprinkle the topping over the poke bowls to serve.

A FLASH IN THE PAN
If you don't want to eat your fish raw, flash-fry it quickly in a skillet before adding to your dish.

PER SERVING: 399 CALS | 15.4G FAT | 2.2G SAT FAT | 45.5G CARBS | 2.4G SUGARS | 5.3G FIBER | 20.4G PROTEIN | 520MG SODIUM

CHICKEN NOODLE PROTEIN SOUP

This classic chicken soup is an easy, nutritious lunch and can be made in advance. It's full of health benefits—red chiles lower cholesterol and soba noodles are made from gluten-free buckwheat flour.

SERVES: 4
PREP: 20 MINS   COOK: 20 MINS

4¼ cups chicken broth
1 tablespoon soy sauce
1 garlic clove, crushed
1 red chile, seeded and finely chopped
1¼-inch piece fresh ginger, peeled and grated
1 pound 2 ounces skinless, boneless chicken breasts
4 eggs
14 ounces soba noodles
⅔ cup corn kernels
4 small bok choys, cut lengthwise into quarters
1 tablespoon sesame oil, for drizzling

1. Put the broth, soy sauce, garlic, chile, and ginger into a saucepan and bring to a boil. Add the chicken and simmer for 10–12 minutes, until the chicken is tender and the juices run clear when the tip of a sharp knife is inserted into the thickest part of the meat. Remove the chicken with a slotted spoon.

2. Meanwhile, boil the eggs for 4–5 minutes in a saucepan of boiling water. Refresh under cold water. Drain and peel the eggs.

3. Return the broth to the heat, bring to a simmer, and add the noodles. Cook for 2 minutes, or according to the package directions. Add the corn and bok choy, and simmer for an additional 2 minutes.

4. Shred or thickly slice the chicken and return to the pan with the broth and noodles to heat through for 1 minute.

5. Serve the soup in four warm bowls with halved soft-boiled eggs on top and drizzled with the sesame oil.

WHY NOT TRY?
You can make this soup with a mixture of fish broth, white fish, and shrimp if you don't want chicken.

PER SERVING: 677 CALS | 14.3G FAT | 3.3G SAT FAT | 80.7G CARBS | 12.2G SUGARS | 5G FIBER | 52.7G PROTEIN | 1,200MG SODIUM

ZUCCHINI AND BEAN TACOS

*Tacos and homemade guacamole can be a delicious snack
or light lunch. This recipe includes a salad made with cannellini
beans for protein, plus crunchy celery, carrot, and zucchini for extra fiber.*

SERVES: 4
PREP: 12 MINS, PLUS COOLING   COOK: 30 MINS

TACO SHELLS
2 zucchini, grated
1⅓ cups freshly grated Parmesan cheese
2 cups fresh bread crumbs
2 eggs, beaten
salt and pepper (optional)

GUACAMOLE
1 red chile, seeded and finely diced
juice of ½ lime
2 ripe avocados, pitted and peeled

TACO FILLING
2 celery stalks, thinly sliced
1 zucchini, diced
1 carrot, peeled and grated
1 small red onion, peeled and diced
3 cups drained and rinsed, canned cannellini beans
8 cherry tomatoes, quartered
2 tablespoons chopped fresh cilantro
2 tablespoons extra virgin olive oil

TO SERVE
1 cup fresh watercress
¼ cup plain yogurt
2 tablespoons pumpkin seeds, toasted

1. Preheat the oven to 400°F. Line two baking sheets with nonstick parchment paper and set aside.

2. To make the taco shells, wrap the grated zucchini in paper towels and squeeze as much moisture from them as possible. Mix the zucchini, cheese, bread crumbs, and eggs together in a bowl. Season with salt and pepper, if using.

3. Spread the mixture into eight circles on the prepared baking sheets. Bake in the preheated oven for 20 minutes.

4. Turn the taco shells over and bake for an additional 10 minutes, then remove from the baking sheets and lay over a rolling pin to help them curl. Let cool.

5. Meanwhile, make the guacamole. Put the chile, lime juice, and avocados into a small bowl and mash together until smooth. Set aside.

6. To make the taco filling, mix together the celery, zucchini, carrot, onion, beans, tomatoes, cilantro, and olive oil in a bowl.

7. Divide the watercress among the cooled taco shells, then spoon the bean mixture into each one.

8. Top each taco with a dollop of guacamole and yogurt, and sprinkle with toasted pumpkin seeds to serve.

HEALTHY ZUCCHINI
Zucchini provide immune system–boosting vitamin C and significant levels of potassium, which help control blood pressure.

PER SERVING: 621 CALS | 33G FAT | 9.3G SAT FAT | 50.3G CARBS | 10.6G SUGARS | 17.4G FIBER | 31.2G PROTEIN | 640MG SODIUM

BLACK RICE AND POMEGRANATE BOWL

This colorful bowl is full of flavor and bursting with protein-rich lima beans, black rice, and cottage cheese. Kale and butternut squash also provide antioxidants to keep you happy and healthy.

SERVES: 4
PREP: 15 MINS   COOK: 25 MINS

1 small butternut squash, peeled, seeded and diced
1 red onion, peeled and sliced
1 tablespoon olive oil
2/3 cup black rice
1 cup shredded kale
2 tablespoons pine nuts
1²/₃ cups drained and rinsed, canned lima beans
1/4 cup cottage cheese, to serve
seeds from 1 pomegranate, to serve

DRESSING
1/4 cup tahini paste
juice of 1 lemon
1 garlic clove, crushed
2 tablespoons extra virgin olive oil

1. Preheat the oven to 400°F.

2. Put the butternut squash and onion onto a roasting pan and drizzle with the olive oil. Roast in the preheated oven for 15 minutes.

3. Cook the rice according to the package directions.

4. Meanwhile, add the kale and pine nuts to the squash and roast for an additional 10 minutes. Remove from the oven and toss in the lima beans.

5. To make the dressing, whisk the tahini, lemon juice, garlic, and olive oil together in a small bowl. Set aside.

6. Drain the rice and divide among four warm bowls. Spoon the roasted vegetables and nuts over the rice, and add a dollop of cottage cheese and sprinkling of pomegranate seeds.

7. Drizzle the dressing into each bowl to serve.

VITAMIN C BOOST
For even more color and extra vitamin C, add red and yellow bell peppers to the roasting pan with the squash.

PER SERVING: 492 CALS | 23.7G FAT | 3.3G SAT FAT | 58.7G CARBS | 10.7G SUGARS | 10.5G FIBER | 14.8G PROTEIN | 80MG SODIUM

PINK
ENERGY BARS

The fun hidden ingredient in these bars is the beet. Beets are an excellent source of folate and is full of magnesium, fiber, vitamin C, iron, vitamin B6, manganese, potassium, and copper—a bundle of goodness!

MAKES: 10 BARS
PREP: 6 MINS, PLUS CHILLING   COOK: NONE

½ cup rolled oats
½ cup ground almonds (almond meal)
2 tablespoons smooth peanut butter
1 small cooked beet
1 tablespoon maple syrup

1. Put the oats into a food processor and process until broken down.

2. Add the remaining ingredients to the processor and process again until the mixture comes together.

3. Press the dough into a 5-inch square pan and smooth the top. Chill in the refrigerator for 1 hour, then cut into bars.

SWEET ENOUGH?
If you're in the mood for something a little less sweet, omit the maple syrup and add salt and pepper instead.

PER BAR: 76 CALS | 4.6G FAT | 0.6G SAT FAT | 7.1G CARBS | 2.4G SUGARS | 1.4G FIBER | 2.6G PROTEIN | TRACE SODIUM

WHOLE-WHEAT LINGUINE WITH MARINATED TOFU

Tofu is a soy-base protein that can be used in stir-fries and other vegetarian dishes. It doesn't have a strong flavor, so making a marinade with garlic, honey, and chile makes it even tastier.

SERVES: 4

PREP: 15 MINS, PLUS MARINATING   COOK: 15 MINS

¾ cup tofu cubes
12 ounces whole-wheat linguine
1 tablespoon olive oil, for frying
2 cups sliced cremini mushrooms
2 fresh thyme sprigs, leaves only
juice of ½ lemon
salt and pepper (optional)
2 tablespoons chopped fresh parsley, to garnish
2 tablespoons freshly grated Parmesan cheese, to garnish

MARINADE
1 tablespoon olive oil
juice and zest of ½ lime
1 garlic clove, crushed
¼ teaspoon crushed red pepper flakes
2 tablespoons soy sauce
2 tablespoons honey

1. To make the marinade, mix all the marinade ingredients together in a large bowl. Add the cubes of tofu, making sure each piece is coated in the mixture. Let marinate for at least 30 minutes.

2. Cook the linguine according to the package directions.

3. Meanwhile, heat the olive oil in a skillet and cook the mushrooms for 5–6 minutes over medium heat. Toss in the thyme leaves and lemon juice just before removing from the heat.

4. Heat a ridged grill pan until hot and cook the tofu over medium heat for 5–6 minutes, until golden.

5. Drain the pasta and transfer it to a large bowl with the mushroom mixture and tofu. Season with salt and pepper, if using. Toss together.

6. Serve the pasta garnished with chopped parsley and grated cheese.

MARVELOUS MUSHROOMS
Mushrooms are an ideal source of healthy protein for vegetarians and vegans.

PER SERVING: 463 CALS | 12.2G FAT | 2G SAT FAT | 77.6G CARBS | 12.3G SUGARS | 8.7G FIBER | 18.1G PROTEIN | 480MG SODIUM

BROILED CHICKEN
AND SLAW BOWL

Here's a perfect midweek meal for essential protein and energy, with crunchy vegetables drizzled in a spicy mayonnaise and topped with tender slices of chicken.

SERVES: 4

PREP: 18 MINS   COOK: 8–10 MINS

4 boneless, skinless chicken breasts, about 5½ ounces each
1 teaspoon smoked paprika
salt and pepper (optional)
12 fresh arugula leaves, to garnish

COLESLAW
2 carrots, peeled and shredded
1 fennel bulb, trimmed and thinly sliced
1 beet, grated
1½ cups shredded red cabbage
15½ cups shredded green cabbage
4 radishes, thinly sliced
1 red onion, peeled and thinly sliced
¼ cup chopped fresh mixed herbs, such as parsley, dill, mint, and cilantro
juice of 1 lemon
2 tablespoons extra virgin olive oil
1 cup plain yogurt
1 tablespoon whole-grain mustard

1. Preheat the broiler to medium heat.

2. To make the coleslaw, put all the coleslaw ingredients into a large bowl. Toss together well and set aside.

3. Place the chicken breasts between two sheets of wax paper and flatten with a rolling pin or mallet to a thickness of ½–¾ inch.

4. Season the chicken with paprika, and salt and pepper, if using. Broil for 4–5 minutes on each side, until the chicken is tender and the juices run clear when the tip of a sharp knife is inserted into the thickest part of the meat.

4. Divide the coleslaw among four bowls and top with slices of chicken breast and the arugula.

DID YOU KNOW?
Flattening the chicken breasts helps them to cook more quickly and evenly. Remove the skin, because this is where the fat is hidden.

PER SERVING: 362 CALS | 13.4G FAT | 3.1G SAT FAT | 21.9G CARBS | 12.7G SUGARS | 6.1G FIBER | 39.2G PROTEIN | 200MG SODIUM

PAN-FRIED TUNA WITH SEAWEED PESTO

You may associate seaweed with Japanese cuisine, but it's actually a versatile ingredient. It's highly nutritious and one of the few ingredients that's rich in iodine, which is important for thyroid health.

SERVES: 4
PREP: 20 MINS   COOK: 25 MINS

4 tuna steaks, about 5½ ounces each
4 teaspoons black pepper
1 tablespoon olive oil
2 cups fresh watercress

SWEET POTATO WEDGES
2 sweet potatoes, cut into wedges
3 tablespoons olive oil
¼ teaspoon smoked paprika
salt and pepper (optional)

SEAWEED PESTO
1½ cups dried wakame, soaked in water
for 20 minutes, until rehydrated, drained
½ garlic clove, chopped
2½ tablepsoons toasted pine nuts
3 tablespoons grated pecorino cheese
juice of ½ lemon
⅓ cup extra virgin olive oil

1. Preheat the oven to 400°F.

2. To make the sweet potato wedges, toss the sweet potato wedges in a bowl with the olive oil and paprika. Season with salt and pepper, if using, then spread across a baking sheet or roasting pan.

3. Roast the sweet potato in the preheated oven for 15–20 minutes, until tender.

4. Meanwhile, make the seaweed pesto. Put the rehydrated wakame into a food processor with the garlic and pine nuts, and process to break down.

5. Add the cheese and lemon juice to the processor and pulse again.

6. With the machine running, slowly add the extra virgin olive oil until you have a pesto consistency. Transfer to a bowl and set aside.

7. Season each tuna steak with 1 teaspoon of black pepper. Make sure both sides are seasoned.

8. Heat the olive oil in a skillet and cook the tuna over high heat for 3–4 minutes on each side, depending on how pink you prefer it.

9. Serve the pan–fried tuna with a dollop of seaweed pesto, the sweet potato wedges, and watercress.

SWEET POTATO POWER
Sweet potatoes are richer in nutrients than potatoes and lower on the glycemic index.

PER SERVING: 602 CALS | 41.4G FAT | 6G SAT FAT | 17.1G CARBS | 3.1G SUGARS | 2.8G FIBER | 40.2G PROTEIN | 240MG SODIUM

MIXED BEAN, NUT, AND KALE STEW

Kale is a wonderfully nourishing vegetable, rich in vitamin B6, fiber, potassium, magnesium, and more. Served with protein-packed beans, this is a dinner the entire family will enjoy.

SERVES: 4
PREP: 10 MINS   COOK: 30 MINS

1 tablespoon olive oil, for sautéing
1 large onion, peeled and chopped
2 garlic cloves, peeled and sliced
1 teaspoon smoked paprika
$1^{1}/_{3}$ cups fava beans
$1^{2}/_{3}$ cups drained and rinsed, canned lima beans
1 cup trimmed and halved green beans
$1^{2}/_{3}$ cups canned diced tomatoes
1 cup vegetable broth
2 cups shredded kale
2 tablespoons chopped walnuts
1 tablespoon chopped Brazil nuts
1 tablespoon chopped hazelnuts
1 cup crumbled feta cheese
salt and pepper (optional)
1 tablespoon chopped fresh mint, to garnish
1 tablespoon extra virgin olive oil, to serve

1. Heat the olive oil in a large saucepan and sauté the onion over medium heat for 2–3 minutes. Stir in the garlic and paprika, and cook for an additional minute.

2. Stir the beans, tomatoes, and broth into the pan and bring to a simmer. Cook for 15 minutes, then stir in the kale and cook for an additional 10 minutes. Season with salt and pepper, if using.

3. Toast the nuts in a dry saucepan over medium heat for 2–3 minutes.

4. Ladle the stew into four bowls and serve topped with the toasted nuts, feta, chopped mint, and a drizzle of olive oil.

COOK'S TIP
If you can get fava beans in season, they are preferable for this recipe. If not, substitute with frozen fava beans.

PER SERVING: 408 CALS | 23.1G FAT | 8.4G SAT FAT | 30.5G CARBS | 9.7G SUGARS | 10.1G FIBER | 19.5G PROTEIN | 600MG SODIUM

BLACK RICE PUDDING

Black rice turns a classic pudding into a stylish, contemporary dish. A great source of iron, vitamin E, and antioxidants, it's also higher in fiber and protein than white or brown rice.

SERVES: 4
PREP: 8 MINS   COOK: 25 MINS

¾ cup black rice
½ cup soy light cream
1 thick slice fresh pineapple, halved
6 knobs preserved ginger, diced
¼ cup preserve ginger syrup
⅓ cup shredded fresh mint leaves
¼ cup coconut yogurt

1. Cook the rice according to the package directions.

2. Drain the rice and put three-quarters of it into a food processor with the soy cream and half the pineapple. Process until you have the consistency of rice pudding.

3. Spoon the rice mixture into four glasses.

4. Dice the remaining pineapple and put into a bowl with the diced ginger, syrup, and mint. Mix well.

5. Spoon the coconut yogurt over the rice mixture, then pour over the ginger-and-pineapple mixture to serve.

PERFECT PINEAPPLE
Pineapples are a good source of vitamin C and other vitamins and minerals, including magnesium.

PER SERVING: 277 CALS | 6.9G FAT | 3.2G SAT FAT | 48.3G CARBS | 15.3G SUGARS | 3G FIBER | 5.7G PROTEIN | TRACE SODIUM

FROZEN YOGURT BARK

*If you're struggling to think of healthy treats for your children,
this frozen yogurt dessert makes a great after-school snack and will
replace potato chips and candy with an assortment of fruits and nuts.*

SERVES: 4

PREP: 10 MINS, PLUS FREEZING   COOK: NONE

2 cups Greek-style yogurt
2 tablespoons maple syrup
zest of 1 orange
1/3 cup blueberries
1/3 cup dried cherries
3/4 cup coarsely chopped pistachio nuts
3/4 cup raspberries

1. Line a 6¼ x 10½-inch shallow baking pan with parchment paper, leaving extra paper hanging over the rim (this will help you lift the bark out once frozen). Set aside.

2. Put the yogurt, maple syrup, orange zest, blueberries, and cherries into a large bowl and mix together.

3. Pour the yogurt mixture into the prepared pan and make sure the fruit is evenly dispersed.

4. Sprinkle the chopped pistachio nuts and raspberries on top of the yogurt. Freeze for at least 2 hours, or until completely frozen.

5. Remove the bark from the pan with the overhanging pieces of paper and cut into shapes of your choice.

INCREASED POWER

To increase the protein content, you could stir some nut butter through the yogurt.

PER SERVING: 349 CALS | 17.9G FAT | 6G SAT FAT | 33.4G CARBS | 23.5G SUGARS | 5G FIBER | 16.9G PROTEIN | 40MG SODIUM

CHOCOLATE YOGURT POPS

Instead of buying sugar-laden ice pops, make these naturally sweet chocolate yogurt pops. They'll be a huge success on hot summer days.

MAKES: 10 POPS
PREP: 20 MINS, PLUS FREEZING   COOK: NONE

1⅓ cups Greek-style yogurt
2 bananas, peeled and mashed
4 teaspoons honey
10½ ounces semisweet chocolate, chopped
½ cup coconut oil
3½ ounces milk chocolate, chopped
3½ ounces white chocolate, chopped
1 tablespoon chopped pistachio nuts

YOU WILL ALSO NEED:
10 (3-ounce) ice pop molds
10 ice pop sticks

1. Put the yogurt into a bowl with the mashed banana and honey. Mix well.

2. Pour the yogurt mixture into ten 3-ounce ice pop molds. Insert the ice pop sticks and freeze for at least 2 hours.

3. Gently melt the semisweet chocolate and coconut oil in a heatproof bowl placed over a saucepan of simmering water. Don't let the bowl touch the water.

4. Melt the milk chocolate in the same way as the semisweet chocolate.

5. Remove the ice pops from the molds and dip them into the melted semisweet chocolate-and-coconut oil mixture, then return to the freezer for a couple of minutes to set.

6. To decorate the ice pops, swirl the melted milk chocolate around each one with a fork, then sprinkle with white chocolate and pistachio nuts. Return to the freezer to set.

DID YOU KNOW?
Bananas are antacids, lowering the distress associated with heartburn, stomachaches, and acid reflux.

PER POP: 438 CALS | 29.7G FAT | 19.9G SAT FAT | 36.7G CARBS | 28.5G SUGARS | 3.5G FIBER | 6.5G PROTEIN | 40MG SODIUM

CHOCOLATE AND ALMOND BISCOTTI

Biscotti are Italian cookies baked twice for a crunchy coating that are traditionally served with coffee. These are made with almonds for protein, calcium, and potassium, and they are decorated with chocolate drizzle.

MAKES: 22 BISCOTTI
PREP: 15 MINS   COOK: 50–60 MINS

1 teaspoon baking powder
1¼ cups all-purpose flour
¾ cup buckwheat flour
¾ cup superfine or granulated sugar
¼ cup cacao powder
¼ teaspoon ground cinnamon
4 eggs, beaten
1¼ cups blanched almonds, toasted and coarsely chopped
3½ ounces semisweet chocolate, to decorate
3½ ounces white chocolate, to decorate

1. Preheat the oven to 300°F. Line a baking sheet with parchment paper and set aside.

2. Put the baking powder, flours, sugar, cacao powder, and cinnamon into a large bowl and stir together.

3. Add the eggs to the bowl and stir into the dry ingredients, adding the almonds once the dough starts coming together.

4. Turn the dough out onto a floured work surface and roll it into a long log shape, about 14 inches long and 2½–2¾ inches wide. Place on the prepared baking sheet and bake in the preheated oven for 30–40 minutes.

5. Remove the sheet from the oven and cool on a rack for 10 minutes.

6. Cut the dough into ½-inch-thick slices and bake for an additional 8–10 minutes on each side, until firm. Cool on a rack.

7. Gently melt the semisweet chocolate and white chocolate in separate heatproof bowls set over saucepans of simmering water. Don't let the bowls touch the water. Once melted, drizzle lines of chocolate over the biscotti to decorate. Let set before serving.

WHY NOT TRY?
Add dried fruits, such as cranberries or chopped apricots, for extra sweetness.

PER BISCOTTI: 178 CALS | 8.6G FAT | 2.6G SAT FAT | 22.3G CARBS | 11.7G SUGARS | 2.2G FIBER | 4.7G PROTEIN | 40MG SODIUM

PEANUT BUTTER AND BANANA MUFFINS

These lovely muffins are healthier than most store-bought ones and can be eaten as a guilt-free dessert after dinner or taken to work for an easy breakfast.

MAKES: 12 MUFFINS

PREP: 12 MINS   COOK: 15–20 MINS

$1^2/_3$ cups all-purpose flour
$^1/_3$ cup plus 1 tablespoon buckwheat flour
$1^1/_2$ teaspoons baking powder
$^1/_3$ cup superfine or granulated sugar
$^1/_3$ cup rolled oats
2 bananas, peeled and mashed
$^1/_3$ cup chunky peanut butter
2 eggs, beaten
2 tablespoons melted coconut oil
$^1/_2$ cup milk

1. Preheat the oven to 400°F. Line a 12-cup muffin pan with paper liners and set aside.

2. Sift the flours, baking powder, and sugar into a large bowl, then mix in the oats.

3. In a separate bowl, mix the mashed banana and peanut butter with the eggs, melted coconut oil, and milk.

4. Stir the banana mixture into the flour mixture, but do not overmix. The tastiest muffins are made from the lumpiest batter.

5. Spoon the batter into the prepared muffin liners and bake in the preheated oven for 15–18 minutes, until risen and golden.

COOK'S TIP
Almond butter or other nut butters can also be used in this recipe.

PER MUFFIN: 214 CALS | 8.3G FAT | 3.2G SAT FAT | 30.1G CARBS | 10.1G SUGARS | 2.3G FIBER | 6.1G PROTEIN | 240MG SODIUM

LOW SUGAR

WHY GO LOW SUGAR?

Sugar seems to be in almost everything we eat, from TV dinners to natural ingredients, such as fruit and vegetables. It is estimated that many of us consume ten or more teaspoons of sugar every day. The negative impact of this high-sugar diet on our health is increasingly evident in rising levels of obesity.

A sugary diet may also be a factor in causing type-two diabetes, and, for those who have diabetes, a diet low in sugar will also help them maintain a healthy weight and reduce the risk of medical complications. However, the problems are not just limited to weight gain. It is thought that sleep disturbances and mood disorders can also be linked to overindulgence in sugar. Even leaving health issues aside, a sugar binge can quickly be followed by a "crash," where your energy levels plummet, leaving you feeling exhausted.

To understand your overall intake of sugar, you need to look beyond the quantity of table sugar that you use from day to day to the products you buy regularly that have significant amounts of "hidden" sugar. Products with hidden sources of sugar range from ketchup, mayonnaise, and salad dressings to pasta sauces, soup, and fruit-flavored yogurts.

This chapter is about becoming aware of where sugar is found, both openly and concealed, within day-to-day cooking, and then taking action to avoid it. The problems aren't only associated with refined sugars; sugar is sugar after all, and natural sugars need to be restricted, too, especially in the form of fructose.

In this chapter, you'll find low-sugar versions of the things you love to eat, such as a reduced-sugar tomato Italian Meat Sauce on page 170 and Fried Chicken with Spicy Red Cabbage Coleslaw on page 172. However, no one wants their favorite foods adapted so much that they bear no resemblance to the original. If you bake a cake, you want to end up with something that looks and tastes like a cake. The Zucchini Loaf Cake with Cream Cheese Frosting on page 180 is sure to delight cake lovers.

Of course, you probably won't be able to eradicate all sugar from your diet; for example, it would be unrealistic and inadvisable to stop permanently eating all fruit. However, the recipes in this chapter include no more than 6 grams of sugar per 3½ ounces of ingredients. If you keep your intake to this low-to-negligible level, you can be confident that you are managing your sugars well.

WHAT IS FRUCTOSE?

Sugar, or sucrose as it is scientifically known, comes in the chemical forms of glucose and fructose. Glucose is the basic stuff of life, and every single cell in every single thing growing or moving produces and uses it. We do not need to go out of our way to consume glucose, because the body's digestive system releases it from a lot of foods. Fructose is the simplest form of carbohydrate, and is about one-and-one-fifth times the sweetness of table sugar.

Throughout human evolution, fructose has been only periodically available in especially ripe fruit and some vegetables and nuts. The human body can handle small amounts of fructose well, but is not designed to deal with it in large amounts, so it can be damaging if we eat too much. While every cell in the body is slurping up glucose, only the liver can process fructose in significant amounts. If the liver is overloaded with fructose, it converts it straight into fat, which has the result of weight gain and has been linked to obesity, type-two diabetes, heart disease, and even cancer.

Another problem with fructose is that while some natural sugars stimulate the release of insulin in the body, fructose sneaks under our natural radar system. Fructose has a slower rate of uptake than glucose and doesn't make you feel full in the same way. It also contains the hormone grehlin, which keeps us feeling hungry. This results in a tendency to eat a greater number of calories if any part of what you are eating contains fructose. Also, once fructose arrives in the liver, it can provide glycerol, the backbone of fat, and increase fat formation, leading to weight gain and the danger of associated diseases.

Most fructose is consumed in liquid form, such as in sweet and carbonated drinks, so it is not connected to other sources of carbohydrate, which increases any negative metabolic effects. Naturally occurring fruit sugars, in contrast, are bonded together and so the impact of the fructose intake is reduced.

As well as being found naturally in fruit and vegetables, fructose is hiding in many day-to-day foods, from some prepared meals and diet products to sugary beverages. Many of us feel we are making a healthy choice if we reach for an apple or raw carrot, but it is important to limit how much high-sugar fruit and vegetables we eat, too. While they are nutritious, the sugar they contain quickly adds up.

HIDDEN SUGARS

Sugar might not necessarily be as easy to detect as you think it is. Even when you know that a product contains sugar, the amount that it contains can still be surprising. An average can of soft drink is estimated to have around seven teaspoons of sugar, and prepared pasta sauces can include between 6 and 12 grams of sugar per serving.

It is advisable to check the packaging when buying any prepared food products. On the front of the package, it may advertise the food's fat and calorie content, but you usually need to check the back for sugars. Often, when the fat is removed from a product, sugar is added to enhance the flavor. Look for the section labeled "Total Carbohydrate"; beneath that it will specify "Sugars." You should also look for dextrose, honey, glucose, and maltose in the products you are buying—these are variations on sugar and can be equally detrimental to our health.

The best way to effectively control your sugar intake is to prepare homemade food with a good balance of fresh ingredients as often as you can. This way, you will know the exact ingredients that are going into your meals and you can avoid sugar-laden products by carefully checking your food labels.

Yet, even natural foods can have potential pitfalls. Many foods from nature, including most fruit, are full of sugar. If you want to cut out sugar, fruit juice and dried fruit should also be avoided. Vegetables can also have a high sugar content; sugarsnap peas, artichokes, and beets are just some of the vegetables that are high in sugar and should, therefore, be eaten sparingly. It is also true that the natural sugar in some fruit, including apples, has increased as new varieties have been developed to answer our desire for a sweet fix.

If you are eating a product that does not conveniently come with a helpful breakdown of its nutritional components, simply avoid products or ingredients that taste sweet, and remember that "low-calorie" does not necessarily mean "low-sugar."

It is important to look out for refined carbohydrates. The body reacts to most carbohydrates by breaking them down into sugar. White flour, therefore, should be avoided, which means most pastries, breads, and cakes should not be eaten. White rice, noodles, pasta, and potatoes are also off the menu.

GOOD FATS AND PROTEIN

The low-sugar eater has two great allies: protein and fat. Since the 1980s, it has been fashionable to label fat as "the enemy" and carbs as "the good guys." A big bowl of pasta has long been considered a healthy choice. Now, the rise of the low-carb lifestyle has turned these beliefs on their head, and a small portion of whole-wheat pasta is considered a healthy portion. If you're keeping your sugar intake down and avoiding refined carbohydrates, you will need protein and fat to replace this energy.

The body naturally produces leptin to regulate and distribute fat. The body's regulatory gland, the hypothalamus, is sensitive to leptin and will tell the brain the stomach is full when there is leptin in the blood, thus suppressing appetite.

The avocado, a food that is naturally low in sugar but loaded with monounsaturated fats, which play a big role in reducing cholesterol, is a good choice for anyone watching their sugar intake. Heroic monounsaturated fats are found all over the food aisles, in products from olive oil and oily fish to animal fats, nuts, and dairy. These foods often contain virtually no sugar, and so are used as the basis for many low-sugar recipes, adding a sense of indulgence to a dish. Of course, as with everything, it is important to manage your intake of foods containing mono-unsaturated fats; they should be eaten in moderation.

Fat's fondly regarded cousin is protein. Lean meats and eggs can certainly be enjoyed as a low-sugar option. Protein has a marvelous ability to make you feel full; if you eat enough of it, a hormone called PYY is triggered, which is effective in creating a sense of fullness and removing the desire to eat.

Protein-rich products are incredibly diverse. They include meat and fish; dairy products, such as cheese and yogurt; seeds and nuts; and some surprising grains, such as quinoa.

Natural, high-protein ingredients tend to be low in sugar, too. However, watch out for processed products advertising themselves as high protein, because they can also contain hidden sugars used to add extra flavor or texture.

AVOCADO, BACON, AND CHILE FRITTATA

Inspired by the flavors of Mexico, this protein-packed frittata is wonderful lingered over on a lazy morning. You can make it ahead and store it in the refrigerator for up to two days.

SERVES: 4
PREP: 15 MINS   COOK: 14 MINS

1 tablespoon vegetable oil
8 bacon strips, coarsely chopped
6 eggs, beaten
3 tablespoons heavy cream
2 large avocados, peeled and sliced
1 red chile, seeded and thinly sliced
½ lime
sea salt and pepper (optional)

1. Preheat the broiler to medium. Heat the oil in an 8-inch ovenproof skillet over medium heat. Add the bacon and cook, stirring, for 4–5 minutes, or until crisp and golden. Using a slotted spoon, transfer to a plate lined with paper towels. Remove the pan from the heat.

2. Pour the eggs into a bowl, add the cream, and season with salt and pepper, if using, then beat. Return the pan to the heat. When it is hot, pour in the egg mixture and cook for 1–2 minutes, without stirring. Sprinkle the bacon and avocado on top and cook for an additional 2–3 minutes, or until the frittata is almost set and the underside is golden brown.

3. Place the frittata under the preheated broiler and cook for 3–4 minutes, or until the top is golden brown and the egg is set. Sprinkle with the chile and squeeze the lime juice over the top. Cut into wedges and serve.

COOKING BACON

The soft texture of the frittata works best with really crispy bacon. To achieve this, cook the bacon over medium heat until it has a dark golden color, then remove it from the pan and drain on paper towels.

PER SERVING: 525 CALS | 41.6G FAT | 15G SAT FAT | 8.8G CARBS | 1.5G SUGARS | 4.8G FIBER | 23.5G PROTEIN | 1,000MG SODIUM

ZUCCHINI PANCAKES WITH SMOKED SALMON AND SCRAMBLED EGGS

*Zucchini make a beautiful substitute for potatoes in these tasty pancakes;
their subtle creamy flavor complements the luxurious egg and salmon perfectly.*

SERVES: 2
PREP: 30 MINS   COOK: 18 MINS

3 extra-large eggs
1 tablespoon heavy cream
2 teaspoons finely snipped fresh chives
1 tablespoon butter
2 large slices of smoked salmon, to serve
sea salt and pepper (optional)

PANCAKES

1 large zucchini, grated
2 teaspoons quinoa flour
¼ cup grated Parmesan cheese
1 extra-large egg yolk
1 tablespoon heavy cream
1 tablespoon vegetable oil

1. Preheat the oven to 225°F. To make the pancakes, lay a clean kitchen towel on a work surface and pile the zucchini in the center. Holding the kitchen towel over the sink, gather the sides together and twist them tightly until all the liquid from the zucchini has run out.

2. Put the zucchini, flour, Parmesan, egg yolk, and cream into a bowl and mix well. Roll the mixture into two balls and flatten them with the palms of your hands to make thick pancakes.

3. Heat the oil in a small skillet over medium–low heat. Cook the pancakes for 5–8 minutes on each side, or until golden brown. Remove from the heat, transfer to a baking sheet, and put them in the oven to keep warm.

4. To make the scrambled eggs, crack the eggs into a bowl, add the cream and chives, and season with salt and pepper, if using. Beat with a fork until evenly mixed.

5. Wipe the skillet clean with paper towels, then melt the butter in the pan over low heat. Pour in the egg mixture and cook, stirring, for 5–6 minutes, or until the eggs are just set.

6. Put the warm pancakes on two plates. Spoon the scrambled eggs over them, then top with the salmon. Grind over some black pepper, if using, and serve immediately.

PERFECT SCRAMBLED EGGS

When cooking scrambled eggs, the trick any chef will tell you is "low and slow"—keep the heat down and stir patiently until the eggs start to bind. They will keep cooking all the time they're in the pan, so serve them quickly.

PER SERVING: 428 CALS | 33.2G FAT | 13.4G SAT FAT | 7.3G CARBS | 4G SUGARS | 1.6G FIBER | 25G PROTEIN | 880MG SODIUM

CREAMY OATMEAL
WITH BLACKBERRIES

*Oats are complex carbohydrates that provide slow-release energy
to keep you sustained throughout the morning.*

SERVES: 2
PREP: 5 MINS   COOK: 8 MINS

½ cup rolled oats
small pinch of sea salt
2½ cups cold water
¼ cup heavy cream, plus extra to serve
1 tablespoon stevia
1 tablespoon pumpkin seeds
6 large blackberries, quartered

1. Put the oats and salt in a medium saucepan and pour the water over them. Bring to a boil, then reduce the heat to medium-low and simmer, stirring regularly, for 5–6 minutes, or until the oats are thick but have a dense pouring consistency.

2. Stir in the cream and stevia. Spoon the oatmeal into two bowls, top with the pumpkin seeds and blackberries, and serve immediately with a little extra cream for pouring over the top.

ALSO TRY THIS
The Scots have made oatmeal with just water for generations, so you can omit the cream if you prefer. It does, however, provide calcium.

PER SERVING: 268 CALS | 9G FAT | 2.9G SAT FAT | 38G CARBS | 1.5G SUGARS | 7.2G FIBER | 11G PROTEIN | 280MG SODIUM

GREEK-STYLE YOGURT WITH ORANGE ZEST AND TOASTED SEEDS

Toasting the seeds in this recipe enhances their flavor, so they contrast wonderfully with the smooth, creamy yogurt.

SERVES: 2

PREP: 5 MINS   COOK: 3 MINS

2 teaspoons flaxseed
2 teaspoons pumpkin seeds
2 teaspoons chia seeds
1 cup Greek-style plain yogurt
grated zest of 1 small orange, plus 1 teaspoon juice

1. Place a small skillet over medium heat. When it is hot, add the seeds. Toast, stirring constantly with a wooden spoon, until they start to turn brown and release a nutty aroma. Transfer them to a plate and let cool.

2. Spoon the yogurt into two glass jars or serving bowls, then sprinkle the seeds on top, followed by the orange zest. Sprinkle with the orange juice and serve immediately.

FLAXSEED FOR HEALTH
Flaxseed are high in omega-3s, which are essential fatty acids that some studies show can help reduce the risk of heart disease and stroke.

PER SERVING: 172 CALS | 10.6G FAT | 4.3G SAT FAT | 8.1G CARBS | 4.3G SUGARS | 3.3G FIBER | 12G PROTEIN | TRACE SODIUM

RED PEPPER PEP-UP JUICE

Full of disease-fighting, antiaging antioxidants,
this juice provides loads of energy to help you get through the day.

SERVES: 2
PREP: 5 MINS

2 fennel bulbs with leaves, halved
1 apple, halved
1 small red bell pepper, halved
1 carrot, halved
1 cup cold water

1. Remove a few leaves from the fennel and reserve.

2. Feed the apple, followed by the fennel and bell pepper, then the carrot, through a juicer.

3. Pour into a pitcher, add the water, and mix well.

4. Pour into two glasses, garnish with the reserved fennel leaves, and serve immediately.

AMAZING APPLES
Apples are a good source of vitamin C, soluble pectin (which is thought to help lower cholesterol), and the minerals calcium, magnesium, and phosphorus.

PER SERVING: 93 CALS | 0.5G FAT | TRACE SAT FAT | 21.9G CARBS | 10.9G SUGARS | 1.5G FIBER | 2.6G PROTEIN | 80MG SODIUM

SWEET POTATO SOUP

This thick, colorful, and filling soup has a wonderful sweet flavor,
yet the sugar levels are low.

SERVES: 6
PREP: 25 MINS   COOK: 30 MINS

1 tablespoon vegetable oil
1 onion, finely chopped
1-inch piece fresh ginger,
peeled and finely chopped
1 teaspoon medium curry powder
1 teaspoon sea salt
3 sweet potatoes, coarsely chopped
1²/₃ cups coconut milk
3³/₄ cups vegetable stock
juice of 1 lime
2 tablespoons coarsely chopped fresh cilantro,
to garnish

1. Heat the oil in a large, heavy saucepan over medium-high heat. Add the onion and ginger and cook, stirring, for 5 minutes, or until soft. Add the curry powder and salt and cook, stirring, for an additional minute. Add the sweet potatoes, coconut milk, and stock, then bring to a boil. Reduce the heat to medium and simmer, uncovered, for 20 minutes, or until the sweet potatoes are soft.

2. Puree the soup, either in batches in a blender or food processor, or using a handheld immersion blender. Return the soup to the heat, bring back up to a simmer, then stir in the lime juice. Transfer the soup to bowls and sprinkle with the cilantro.

SWEET POTATOES
High in vitamin C, potassium, and beta-carotene (which the body converts to vitamin A), sweet potatoes make a healthy addition to any meal. They are also a source of manganese.

PER SERVING: 242 CALS | 13.3G FAT | 9.8G SAT FAT | 27G CARBS | 7.2G SUGARS | 3.8G FIBER | 3G PROTEIN | 640MG SODIUM

WARM QUINOA, ROASTED SQUASH, AND PINE NUT SALAD

Quinoa is considered a sacred food by the Incas, and has long been prized for its flavor and ability to keep you feeling full. Loaded with protein and vitamins, it is perfect for a salad.

SERVES: 2
PREP: 20 MINS   COOK: 30 MINS

½ cup white quinoa, rinsed
1½ cups cold water
1½ cups peeled and seeded acorn squash, butternut squash, or pumpkin chunks
¼ cup olive oil
pinch of cayenne pepper
2 tablespoons pine nuts
¼ cup coarsely chopped fresh flat-leaf parsley
¾ cup baby spinach
juice of ¼ lemon, plus lemon wedges to serve
sea salt and pepper (optional)

1. Preheat the oven to 350°F. Put the quinoa in a saucepan. Add the water, bring to a boil, then cover and simmer over low heat for 10 minutes. Remove from the heat, but leave the pan covered for an additional 7 minutes to let the grains swell. Fluff up with a fork.

2. Meanwhile, put the squash and 2 tablespoons of oil in a large roasting pan, sprinkle with the cayenne and a pinch of salt, if using, and toss well. Roast for 25 minutes, or until crisp on the edges and tender. Transfer to a large bowl.

3. Toast the pine nuts in a dry skillet over high heat until they are light brown, then transfer to the bowl. Gently mix in the quinoa, parsley, and spinach, being careful that nothing breaks up, then season with salt and pepper, if using.

4. Divide the salad between two plates, drizzle with the remaining oil and the lemon juice, and serve with lemon wedges for squeezing over the salad.

COOKING QUINOA

Cooked quinoa should have a texture similar to slightly chewy couscous, but be careful not to overcook it. If the pan boils dry during cooking, add a splash more water and turn off the heat, then let rest for 10 minutes with the lid on; the trapped steam should be enough to finish cooking the quinoa without saturating it.

PER SERVING: 521 CALS | 37G FAT | 4.5G SAT FAT | 40.5G CARBS | 2G SUGARS | 4.6G FIBER | 9.9G PROTEIN | 600MG SODIUM

FLATBREAD PIZZAS WITH GARLIC ZUCCHINI RIBBONS

This fresh, Mediterranean-style lunch with a satisfying crunchy crust and fresh vegetable topping is sure to keep hunger pangs at bay.

SERVES: 2
PREP: 20 MINS   COOK: 10 MINS

¼ cup crème fraîche (or extra ricotta cheese)
1 zucchini, shredded into ribbons
using a vegetable peeler
4 cherry tomatoes, quartered
¼ cup ricotta cheese
1 garlic clove, crushed
2 tablespoons olive oil
salad greens, to serve (optional)

PIZZA CRUSTS
¾ cup whole-wheat flour, plus extra to dust
⅓ cup quinoa flour
¾ teaspoon baking soda
1 tablespoon olive oil
2 tablespoons warm water
sea salt (optional)

1. Preheat the oven to 400°F. To make the pizza crusts, put the flours and baking soda in a mixing bowl, season with salt, if using, and stir. Add the oil, then gradually mix in enough of the warm water to make a soft but not sticky dough.

2. Lightly dust a work surface with flour. Knead the dough on the surface for 2 minutes, or until smooth and slightly elastic.

3. Put two large, flat baking sheets in the oven to get hot.

4. Divide the dough into two pieces. Roll out each piece to a circle about ¼ inch thick. Remove the hot baking sheets from the oven and, working quickly, lay the dough on top. Spread the crème fraîche over the pizza crusts, then sprinkle with the zucchini and tomatoes. Blob the ricotta cheese in small dollops on top and put the pizzas in the oven.

5. Bake for 7–10 minutes, or until the crust is crispy and slightly puffed up, and the ricotta is tinged golden.

6. Mix the garlic and oil together in a small bowl, then drizzle it over the hot pizzas. Serve with salad greens, if using.

KNEADING DOUGH
Push the dough down, stretching it out in front of you, using the heels of your hands. You are trying to stretch the gluten strands in it. Fold the top half of the dough back toward you and press down and stretch again. Continue like this until the dough is smooth and elastic.

PER SERVING: 568 CALS | 31.4G FAT | 8G SAT FAT | 57.6G CARBS | 3.7G SUGARS | 8.2G FIBER | 14G PROTEIN | 840MG SODIUM

NO-CRUST SQUASH, CHORIZO, AND GOAT CHEESE QUICHE

This simple quiche is brimming with energy-boosting chorizo and vitamin-packed butternut squash—and is ideal for packing into a lunch bag.

SERVES: 4

PREP: 30 MINS   CHILL: 30 MINS   COOK: 1 HOUR 20 MINS

1 butternut squash, peeled, seeded, and diced
1 tablespoon olive oil
7 ounces chorizo, cut into small, irregular chunks
3 eggs
½ cup crème fraîche or sour cream
2 tablespoons fresh thyme leaves
4 ounces semihard goat cheese
sea salt and pepper (optional)
salad greens, to serve (optional)

PASTRY DOUGH

4 tablespoons cold butter, diced
¾ cup whole-wheat flour, plus extra to dust
2 tablespoons cold water

CHILLING DOUGH

Just before you put the wrapped dough in the refrigerator, shape it into a flat-topped disk—like a big burger patty. This will make it easier to roll.

1. Preheat the oven to 375°F. To make the dough, put the butter in a mixing bowl, add the flour, and season with salt and pepper, if using. Rub the butter into the flour until it resembles fine bread crumbs. Alternatively, process it in a food processor. Gradually mix in enough water to make a soft but not sticky dough.

2. Lightly dust a work surface with flour. Pat the dough into a disk (see "Chilling Dough" below), then wrap it in plastic wrap. Chill in the refrigerator for at least 30 minutes.

3. Meanwhile, to make the filling, put the butternut squash and oil in a large roasting pan, season with salt and pepper, if using, and toss well. Roast for 15 minutes, then stir and add the chorizo. Roast for an additional 15 minutes, or until the squash is crisp on the edges and tender, and the chorizo is crisp. Set aside to cool.

4. Dust the work surface with more flour. Knead the dough gently, then roll it out to a circle just under 9 inches in diameter. Place on a baking sheet and prick all over with a fork. Bake for 20 minutes. Remove from the oven and, using the bottom of an 8-inch loose-bottom tart pan as a template, cut a circle in the pastry. Set aside to cool.

5. Meanwhile, crack the eggs into a large bowl and lightly beat with a fork. Stir in the crème fraîche or sour cream and thyme and season with plenty of pepper, if using.

6. Line the 8-inch tart pan with parchment paper. Carefully place your cooled pastry circle in the pan, then sprinkle with the chorizo and butternut squash. Pour the egg mixture over them, then crumble the goat cheese on top. Reduce the oven temperature to 325°F. Bake the quiche for 30 minutes, or until the egg in the center is set. Serve warm or cold, with salad greens, if using.

PER SERVING: 677 CALS | 49.7G FAT | 23.5G SAT FAT | 32G CARBS | 3.9G SUGARS | 4.7G FIBER | 27.5G PROTEIN | 1,200MG SODIUM

SMOKY PAPRIKA SWEET POTATO FRIES WITH SOUR CREAM DIP

Starchy and sweet, with crunchy edges and fluffy insides, these fries make a really satisfying snack. Always use the best paprika you can find.

SERVES: 2
PREP: 10 MINS   COOK: 40 MINS

2 sweet potatoes, unpeeled, scrubbed, and cut into sticks or wedges
2 tablespoons olive oil
1 tablespoon smoked paprika
sea salt and pepper (optional)

SOUR CREAM DIP
4 chives, finely snipped
2/3 cup sour cream

1. Preheat the oven to 350°F. Put the sweet potatoes, oil, and smoked paprika in a large bowl, season with salt and pepper, if using, and toss well.

2. Arrange the sweet potatoes in a single layer on a large baking sheet. Bake for 30–40 minutes, or until crisp.

3. To make the dip, put the chives and sour cream in a bowl and mix. Season with salt and pepper, if using, and divide between two small dipping bowls.

4. Line two larger bowls with paper towels. Transfer the fries to the bowls and serve immediately with the dip.

ALSO TRY THIS
This dip works well with 2 tablespoons of finely chopped fresh flat-leaf parsley instead of chives, or try mixing in 1/2 teaspoon of smoked paprika.

PER SERVING: 399 CALS | 28.4G FAT | 10.4G SAT FAT | 32.8G CARBS | 8.8G SUGARS | 5G FIBER | 4G PROTEIN | 440MG SODIUM

RIB-EYE STEAK, CHIMICHURRI SAUCE, AND MASHED SWEET POTATOES

Chimichurri is an Argentinian herb sauce with a texture similar to coarse pesto. Most regions have a variation on it, such as adding anchovies or removing the chile.

SERVES: 2
PREP: 30 MINS   COOK: 22 MINS

1 tablespoon olive oil
2 rib-eye steaks, 4½ ounces each
½ teaspoon ground cumin
sea salt and pepper (optional)

CHIMICHURRI SAUCE
¼ cup fresh flat-leaf parsley, coarsely chopped
1 tablespoon fresh oregano
3 small garlic cloves, coarsely chopped
½ shallot, coarsely chopped
¼ red chile, seeded and coarsely chopped
3 tablespoons extra virgin olive oil
1 teaspoon red wine vinegar
juice of ¼ lemon

MASHED SWEET POTATOES
2 small sweet potatoes, cut into
¾-inch chunks
1½ tablespoons butter

1. To make the mashed sweet potaotes, cook the sweet potatoes in a large saucepan of lightly salted boiling water (if using salt) for 12–15 minutes, or until soft. Drain, then let steam dry in the pan away from the heat for at least 5 minutes. Using a potato masher, mash the potatoes to a smooth consistency.

2. Meanwhile, to make the chimichurri sauce, put all the ingredients in a food processor, season with salt and pepper, if using, and process until you have a paste of a similar consistency to pesto. Add a little extra olive oil if the mixture appears too thick. Spoon into a serving bowl, cover, and set aside.

3. Return the mashed sweet potatoes to the heat and warm through before stirring in the butter. Season with salt and pepper, if using, and keep warm.

4. Massage the oil into both sides of each steak, then sprinkle with salt, if using, and the cumin. Heat a ridged grill pan over high heat until smoking hot. Cook each steak for 2–3 minutes on each side, or for longer if you prefer it well done. Let the steaks rest for 2 minutes.

5. Serve a steak on each of two plates with the chimichurri sauce spooned over them and the mashed sweet potatoes on the side.

STEAK POWER
Steak is crammed with selenium and zinc and contains moderate amounts of iron and phosphorus. It is also a good source of protein and the B vitamins.

PER SERVING: 691 CALS | 52.8G FAT | 15.7G SAT FAT | 26.4G CARBS | 5.2G SUGARS | 3.8G FIBER | 27G PROTEIN | 800MG SODIUM

ITALIAN MEAT SAUCE

A rich, filling, traditional Italian sauce that tastes delicious served stirred into whole-wheat tagliatelle.

SERVES: 4

PREP: 10 MINS   COOK: 1¼ HOURS

1 ounce dried porcini
½ cup lukewarm water
1 tablespoon butter
2 ounces pancetta, diced
1 small onion, finely chopped
1 garlic clove, finely chopped
2 small carrots, finely chopped
2 celery stalks, finely chopped
10½ ounces ground beef
pinch of freshly grated nutmeg
1 tablespoon tomato paste
½ cup red wine
1 cup tomato puree or sauce
2 tablespoons finely chopped fresh flat-leaf parsley
sea salt and pepper (optional)
1 pound fresh whole-wheat tagliatelle (optional)

1. Soak the porcini in the water for 20 minutes, then drain well, reserving the soaking water.

2. Meanwhile, melt the butter in a heavy saucepan over medium heat. Add the pancetta and sauté, stirring, for 4 minutes, or until cooked.

3. Add the onion and garlic and sauté for 4 minutes, or until translucent. Add the carrots and celery, and cook for an additional few minutes, stirring often.

4. Add the ground beef and cook, stirring constantly, for 5 minutes, or until browned. Season with salt and pepper, if using, and add the nutmeg. Stir in the tomato paste and cook for 1–2 minutes, then pour in the wine and tomato puree or sauce.

5. Thinly slice the porcini, then add them to the sauce. Pour in the soaking water through a fine strainer. Cook for 1 hour, or until you have a thickened sauce and the beef is cooked.

6. Meanwhile, cook the tagliatelle, if using, according to the package directions, then drain well. Sprinkle the sauce with the parsley and serve with the tagliatelle, if using.

CHOICE OF PASTA
Italians traditionally serve this Italian meat sauce with tagliatelle, not spaghetti.

PER SERVING: 272 CALS | 11G FAT | 5.1G SAT FAT | 14.6G CARBS | 5G SUGARS | 3G FIBER | 21G PROTEIN | 640MG SODIUM

FRIED CHICKEN WITH SPICY RED CABBAGE COLESLAW

Instead of the usual bread crumbs, this chicken has a really crunchy coating of cornmeal, quinoa flour, and whole-wheat flour, which works well with the zingy coleslaw.

SERVES: 4
PREP: 20 MINS PLUS MARINATING   COOK: 35 MINS

1 cup sour cream
1/2 teaspoon cayenne pepper
1 garlic clove, crushed
4 chicken thighs and 4 chicken drumsticks (about 2 pounds)
2 teaspoons cornmeal
2 tablespoons quinoa flour
2 tablespoons whole-wheat flour
oil for deep frying
sea salt and pepper (optional)

COLESLAW
2 cups shredded red cabbage
1 fennel bulb, shredded
1 red chile, seeded and thinly sliced lengthwise
1/2 cup Greek-style plain yogurt
juice of 1/4 lemon

1. Put the sour cream, cayenne, and garlic in a large bowl and season well with salt and pepper, if using. Add the chicken and toss well. Cover the bowl with plastic wrap and chill in the refrigerator for 2–3 hours, or overnight if you have time.

2. To make the coleslaw, put all the ingredients in a large bowl and toss well, then season with salt and pepper, if using. Cover and chill in the refrigerator.

3. Mix together the cornmeal and flours on a plate and season with salt and pepper, if using. Fill a heavy skillet halfway with oil and place it over medium-high heat. Heat the oil to 350°F, or until a cube of bread browns in 30 seconds. While it heats, sprinkle the flour mixture over the chicken.

4. Cook the chicken in two batches, because too much chicken in the pan will make the oil temperature drop. Using tongs, carefully place half the chicken in the oil. Cook for 6–8 minutes, then turn and cook for an additional 6–8 minutes, until the coating is a deep golden brown, the chicken is cooked through to the bone, and the juices run clear with no sign of pink when the tip of a sharp knife is inserted into the thickest part of the meat.

5. Using a slotted spoon, transfer the cooked chicken to paper towels to drain, then keep warm in a low oven while you cook the second batch.

6. Serve the chicken on a sharing board with the coleslaw.

PER SERVING: 695 CALS | 47.4G FAT | 14.5G SAT FAT | 30G CARBS | 6G SUGARS | 6G FIBER | 38G PROTEIN | 520MG SODIUM

MONKFISH IN PESTO AND PROSCIUTTO WITH RICOTTA SPINACH

Monkfish can dry out during cooking, but by wrapping it in prosciutto, you can keep it moist and add plenty of extra flavor and texture.

SERVES: 4
PREP: 25 MINS   COOK: 25 MINS

8 prosciutto slices
3 tablespoons fresh green pesto
8 large fresh basil leaves
1¼ pounds monkfish tail, separated into 2 fillets
1 tablespoon olive oil

RICOTTA SPINACH
2 tablespoons olive oil
1 garlic clove, thinly sliced
5½ cups baby spinach
2 tablespoons ricotta cheese
sea salt and pepper (optional)

1. Preheat the oven to 350°F. Lay two large sheets of plastic wrap side–by–side on a work surface. Arrange the prosciutto slices on the plastic wrap so the long sides overlap by ½ inch. Spread the pesto all over the ham, leaving a ¾–inch border around the edge. Sprinkle the basil over the top.

2. Put one monkfish fillet on top of the pesto and basil, then lay the other fillet next to it the other way around, so its thick end is against its neighbor's thin end.

3. Fold the ham over the ends of the fish and then, using the plastic wrap, roll and encase the whole fillet tightly in the ham. Remove the plastic wrap. Transfer the package to a roasting pan so the seam in the ham is on the bottom, and lightly drizzle with the oil. Roast for 20–25 minutes, or until cooked through but still moist. Cover the pan with aluminum foil to keep the fish warm.

4. To make the ricotta spinach, heat the oil in a large skillet over medium–high heat. Add the garlic and cook for 30 seconds, or until it is soft but not burned. Stir in the spinach and cook, stirring all the time so the oil coats the leaves, for 1 minute, or until it is wilted but not completely collapsed. Transfer to a serving bowl, dot with blobs of the ricotta, and season well with salt and pepper, if using.

5. Place the fish on a serving plate, carve into slices, and pour over any cooking juices from the roasting pan. Serve with the spinach.

MMM, MONKFISH
Monkfish is loaded with protein and includes vitamins B6 and B12, which are essential for brain function. It also includes the minerals phosphorus and selenium.

PER SERVING: 341 CALS | 22G FAT | 5G SAT FAT | 2.5G CARBS | 0.6G SUGARS | 0.8G FIBER | 35.2G PROTEIN | 920MG SODIUM

BAKED PUMPKIN AND CHEESE

This creamy, wholesome dip served in a pumpkin shell is loads of fun and will be loved by the whole family.

SERVES: 4
PREP: 15 MINS   COOK: 1 HOUR 10 MINS

1 small pumpkin
1¼ cups heavy cream
3 garlic cloves, thinly sliced
1 tablespoon fresh thyme leaves, plus sprigs to garnish
4½ ounces Gruyère, Swiss, or Muenster cheese
sea salt and pepper (optional)
4 slices of whole-grain crusty bread, to serve
2½ cups peppery salad greens, such as watercress or mâche, to serve (optional)

1. Preheat the oven to 350°F. Cut horizontally straight through the top quarter of the pumpkin to form a lid. Scoop out the seeds. Put the pumpkin in a large, deep ovenproof dish.

2. Put the cream and garlic in a saucepan, then place it over medium heat and bring to just below boiling point. Remove from the heat, season with salt and pepper, if using, and stir in the thyme. Pour the mixture into the pumpkin and replace the pumpkin lid.

3. Bake for 1 hour, or until the flesh is tender. Be careful not to overcook the pumpkin, or it may collapse. Remove from the oven, lift off the lid, and sprinkle in the cheese. Bake for an additional 10 minutes with the lid off.

4. Sprinkle with the thyme sprigs and some of the salad, if using. Serve the soft pumpkin flesh with a generous helping of the cheesy cream, a slice of the bread, and the remaining salad, if using.

PUMPKIN POWER
Pumpkin is rich in beta-carotene, which the body converts into vitamin A, a powerful antioxidant that helps us maintain good skin and sight. It is also a good source of the B vitamins, including B_6 and folates.

PER SERVING: 453 CALS | 38G FAT | 23.3G SAT FAT | 18.4G CARBS | 3.5G SUGARS | 1.2G FIBER | 13.3G PROTEIN | 720MG SODIUM

KEY LIME DESSERTS

*Small and rich, these decadent chocolate and zesty lime desserts
make a rich yet surprisingly refreshing end to a meal.*

SERVES: 4

PREP: 10 MINS   COOK: 8 MINUTES   CHILL: 4 HOURS

1 cup heavy cream
1½ tablespoons rice malt syrup
1 ounce bittersweet chocolate,
broken into pieces
finely grated zest of 1 lime, plus 1½ tablespoons juice
1 teaspoon unsweetened cocoa powder

1. Put the cream in a saucepan and slowly bring to a boil over medium heat. Add the rice malt syrup and stir well, then boil for 3 minutes. Stir in the chocolate, most of the lime zest, and all the lime juice until the chocolate has melted.

2. Pour the mixture into four espresso cups. Cover with plastic wrap and chill in the refrigerator for at least 4 hours.

3. Decorate the desserts with the cocoa powder and remaining lime zest and serve.

> **ALSO TRY THIS**
> If you would prefer these desserts a little less rich, then omit the chocolate.

PER SERVING: 276 CALS | 26G FAT | 16.3G SAT FAT | 9.4G CARBS | 3.8G SUGARS | 1G FIBER | 2G PROTEIN | TRACE SODIUM

ZUCCHINI LOAF CAKE WITH CREAM CHEESE FROSTING

Zucchini cake is just as delicious as carrot cake. It's super-moist, with a creamy and fresh flavor.

SERVES: 10
PREP: 25 MINS   COOK: 1 HOUR

1³/₄ cups ground almonds (almond meal)
¹/₂ teaspoon baking powder
¹/₂ teaspoon baking soda
3 tablespoons stevia
¹/₃ cup chopped mixed nuts
4 tablespoons butter
2 extra-large eggs, beaten
1 teaspoon vanilla extract
2 cups shredded zucchini

FROSTING
1 cup cream cheese
1 tablespoon stevia
finely grated zest and juice of ¹/₄ unwaxed lemon

1. Preheat the oven to 325°F. Line a nonstick loaf pan with parchment paper.

2. Put the ground almonds, baking powder, baking soda, stevia, and half the nuts in a large bowl and stir well.

3. Melt the butter in a small saucepan over medium-low heat. Pour it onto the dry ingredients. Add the eggs, vanilla, and zucchini, and mix well.

4. Spoon the batter into the prepared pan and spread it into an even layer. Bake for 55–60 minutes, or until well risen and a toothpick comes out clean when inserted into the center of the cake. Let cool for 15 minutes, then remove from the pan, peel off the parchment paper, and transfer to a wire rack.

5. To make the frosting, put the cream cheese and stevia in a large bowl and whisk until light and airy. Add the lemon zest and juice, and whisk again briefly. Using a spatula, spread the frosting over the top of the cake. Decorate with the remaining nuts and serve.

UNWAXED LEMONS
If you are intending to use the zest, it is important to buy unwaxed lemons. If you can't find them, scrub the lemons well before use. Choose firm, heavy lemons with a thick, knobbly skin that has no tinges of green.

PER SERVING: 237 CALS | 21.9G FAT | 6.5G SAT FAT | 5.3G CARBS | 2.2G SUGARS | 2.4G FIBER | 7.2G PROTEIN | 240MG SODIUM

VANILLA PANNA COTTA WITH PISTACHIOS AND ROSEWATER

Panna cotta is an elegant dessert. Here, the dairy milk is replaced by unsweetened almond milk, which complements the fragrant rosewater and emerald pistachios.

SERVES: 4
PREP: 15 MINS   COOK: 4 MINS   CHILL: 2¼ HOURS

3 sheets of gelatin
1¼ cups heavy cream
1 cup unsweetened almond milk
1 vanilla bean, split lengthwise
2 tablespoons stevia
2 tablespoons rosewater
2 tablespoons unsalted pistachio nuts, coarsely chopped

1. Soak the gelatin in a shallow bowl of cold water for 5–10 minutes, or until floppy.

2. Meanwhile, pour the cream and almond milk into a large, heavy saucepan. Scrape in the vanilla seeds using a sharp knife, then drop in the bean. Bring to a boil over medium–high heat, stirring from time to time. Let cool for 5 minutes, then stir in the stevia and, using a fork, remove the vanilla bean.

3. Squeeze the water out of the gelatin and stir the gelatin into the custard until dissolved. Pour the custard into four ramekins (individual ceramic dishes), then let cool for 15 minutes. Cover with plastic wrap and chill in the refrigerator for at least 2 hours, or overnight if you have the time.

4. Fill a bowl halfway with boiling water. Dip each ramekin into the water briefly, making sure it doesn't splash over the top, then turn out onto serving plates. Drizzle the panna cottas with the rosewater and sprinkle with the pistachio nuts.

USING GELATIN
It is important the mixture cools to lukewarm before you add the gelatin; if the heat is too high, the gelatin won't set the dessert. Test it with your finger.

PER SERVING: 313 CALS | 31.1G FAT | 17.6G SAT FAT | 4.2G CARBS | 0.5G SUGARS | 0.8G FIBER | 6.2G PROTEIN | 40MG SODIUM

RASPBERRY AND MASCARPONE ICE CREAM

Fresh raspberries and extra creaminess from the mascarpone mean you will be fighting people off the last scoops of this classic ice cream.

SERVES: 8

PREP: 20 MINS   COOK: 10 MINS   FREEZE: 4 HOURS

1 extra-large egg, plus 4 extra-large egg yolks
2½ tablespoons stevia
½ cup mascarpone cheese
1 teaspoon vanilla extract
1⅔ cups heavy cream
¾ cup raspberries, halved

1. Crack the egg into a large heatproof bowl, add the yolks and stevia, and whisk with an electric handheld mixer for 30 seconds. Place over a saucepan of gently simmering water, making sure the bowl doesn't touch the water, and whisk until the mixture is pale and airy. This cooks the eggs and makes a sweet custard, but be careful not to overcook them.

2. Pour cold water into a bowl and put the custard bowl into it, so the bottom of the custard bowl is cooling in the water. Continue to whisk for 2 minutes, then lift the bowl out of the water and set aside.

3. Put the mascarpone and vanilla in another large bowl and whisk briefly until loose. Pour in the cream and whisk again until it forms soft peaks.

4. Using a metal spoon, gently fold the custard into the cream mixture, preserving as much air as possible. Stir in the raspberries.

5. Pour the mixture into a freezer-proof container, cover with a lid, and freeze for 4 hours, or until set. Take the ice cream out of the freezer 10 minutes before you serve it to let it soften. Scoop it into glasses or small bowls and serve.

ALSO TRY THIS
If you prefer vanilla ice cream, simply omit the raspberries.

PER SERVING: 285 CALS | 28.6G FAT | 16.5G SAT FAT | 3.9G CARBS | 1.2G SUGARS | 0.8G FIBER | 4.2G PROTEIN | 40MG SODIUM

GLUTEN FREE

WHY GO GLUTEN-FREE?

Celiac disease, which is the most common reason to follow a gluten-free diet, affects around 1 in 100 adults worldwide. However, it seems that this is just the tip of a very large iceberg, because some experts believe that only one in eight people with the condition are officially diagnosed, which means many more people may have the condition without knowing it.

However, celiac disease isn't the only reason for going gluten-free, and a growing number of people find that eliminating gluten and wheat can be the answer to a whole range of underlying health problems. Some successful sportspeople have attributed their improved stamina and energy to the fact that they have removed gluten from their diets.

So should you try going gluten-free? Well, if you experience any of the symptoms listed (see right), then it's certainly worth a try—after all, you've got nothing to lose and much to gain.

For people with celiac disease, even the tiniest amount of gluten can cause problems. However, some people with gluten intolerance find they can eat small amounts from time to time.

Cutting gluten out of your meals may seem like a daunting task, but you'll find it doesn't have to be difficult and it doesn't mean missing out on your favorite foods. In this chapter, you'll find delicious recipes for favorites, such as Chicken and Avocado Tacos on page 206 and Apple and Cinnamon Pie on page 222, as well as gluten-free adaptations of other recipes. It will also help you to identify foods you need to avoid and those that might contain hidden gluten, give tips on how to bake with gluten-free flour, and explain how to plan healthy, gluten-free meals that you and your whole family can enjoy.

SYMPTOMS ASSOCIATED WITH CELIAC DISEASE AND GLUTEN INTOLERANCE:

° Digestive problems include diarrhea and/or constipation

° Bloating, stomach pain, cramping

° Unexplained tiredness and lack of energy

° Headaches and migraine

° Canker sores

° Alopecia (hair loss)

° Skin problems

° Painful joints

ELIMINATING GLUTEN

Gluten is a protein found in wheat, rye, and barley, and in foods such as cakes, pastry, bread, and pasta, that are made from these grains. Eliminating gluten from your diet is not as simple as cutting out obvious sources of wheat, such as bread and pasta, because wheat and other gluten-containing grains are often used in other foods.

In some cases, food that is naturally gluten-free can become contaminated with gluten during processing or storage. To make sure a food or ingredient is gluten free, it's vital to check the label on all processed food, or get advice from a celiac advice group about choosing suitable products. It's also important to remember that products that are labeled as wheat-free are not necessarily gluten-free, because they may contain grains such as barley or rye.

FOOD AND BEVERAGES CONTAINING GLUTEN:

° Wheat, rye, barley, and spelt

° All cookies, breads, cakes, chapatis, crackers, muffins, pastries, pizza crusts, rolls, and biscuits made from wheat, rye, spelt, or barley flour

° Wheat noodles and pasta, couscous, semolina, bulgur wheat, farro, and freekeh

° Wheat-base breakfast cereals

° Meat and poultry cooked in batter or bread crumbs, such as ham, chicken, or veal

° Fish or shellfish coated in batter or bread crumbs, such as fish cakes and fish sticks

° Dairy products, such as yogurt, that contain muesli or cereals

° Vegetables and fruit covered in batter or bread crumbs, or dusted with flour

° Potatoes covered in batter or bread crumbs, or dusted with flour, such as potato croquettes

° Soy sauce

° Ice cream cones and wafers and desserts made using semolina or wheat flour

° Stuffing made from bread crumbs

° Barley water/drinks, ale, lager, malted milk, and stout

Check the label on all packaged and processed foods. Avoid foods containing the following ingredients unless you know for sure they are gluten-free:

° Bran, cereal binder, cereal filler, starch, cereal protein, modified starch, edible starch, food starch flour, rusk, rye, and vegetable protein.

GLUTEN-FREE ALTERNATIVES

Cutting out gluten may seem like a huge change, but once you have a routine in place, it will become much easier, and you'll quickly discover that gluten-free meals can be just as delicious as those containing gluten.

There are plenty of foods that are naturally gluten-free and food manufacturers have responded to the growing number of people choosing to avoid gluten by producing a range of products such as gluten-free flour, cakes, cookies, pasta, muffins, pastry, and breads. Of course, you don't need to rely on manufactured gluten-free foods, and our recipes include delicious gluten-free cakes, cookies, and loaves.

HERE ARE SOME NATURALLY GLUTEN-FREE FOODS:

° Gluten-free grains and gluten-free flour—these include amaranth, buckwheat, cassava, chestnut flour, chickpea (besan) flour, cornmeal, corn flour, cornstarch, millet, mustard flour, potato flour, potato starch, quinoa, rice, rice bran, rice flour, sago, sorghum, soy flour, starch, tapioca, tapioca starch, teff, and urd/urid flour

° Meat, poultry, fish, and shellfish

° Fruit and vegetables—canned, dried, fresh, frozen, and juiced pure fruits and vegetables are suitable

° Potatoes, sweet potatoes, rice noodles, buckwheat (soba) noodles (check, because not all brands of buckwheat noodles are gluten-free)

° Nuts and seeds (check dry-roasted peanuts, because they are not always gluten-free)

° Legumes—all dried and canned beans (however, baked beans are not usually gluten-free)

° Dairy products—eggs, cheese, milk, cream, crème fraîche, sour cream, buttermilk, yogurt

° Butter, cooking oils, ghee, lard, margarine, and reduced and low-fat spreads

WHAT ABOUT OATS?

Oats do not contain gluten, but they do contain a similar protein. However, it doesn't seem to cause the same adverse reaction as gluten in wheat and other grains. If you would like to include oats in your diet, start by adding a small amount to see if there is any adverse reaction. Children and people with severe celiac disease are advised to talk to their physician or dietitian before introducing oats into the diet. Oats are often contaminated with gluten during processing, so it's important to make sure you buy oats that are labeled as gluten-free.

THE GLUTEN-FREE KITCHEN

For people with celiac disease and severe gluten intolerance, even the tiniest amount of gluten can be enough to trigger a reaction. So one of the first things you need to do when you switch to a gluten-free diet is to organize your kitchen to minimize the risk of cross-contamination—this is particularly important if you are sharing the kitchen with people who can, and do, eat gluten. You need to create a gluten-free zone.

Just because you can't see gluten, it doesn't mean it's not there. So before you start preparing food, wipe down surfaces and wash all pots and pans thoroughly with detergent and hot water. For utensils and equipment, such as cutting boards, colanders, serving tongs, and wooden spoons, it's helpful to have a set that are used exclusively for gluten-free cooking. Color coding equipment makes it clear which is gluten-free.

If possible, keep all your gluten-free ingredients in a separate cabinet to keep them away from ingredients containing gluten. Careful labeling will help avoid cross-contamination and keep the kitchen a gluten-free zone. Use labels on jars of gluten-free flour and grains. Sticky notes are also useful so you can label your foods in the refrigerator if you share your house with people who consume gluten. It is wise to dedicate one shelf in the refrigerator for gluten-free food—the top shelf is best so you can avoid the risk of something spilling on the food below.

Appliances, such as toasters, can easily become cross-contaminated with gluten, so it is advisable to keep a separate toaster for gluten-free bread. You can also use toaster bags to prevent contamination. If you are planning on making gluten-free bread, it is worth investing in a breadmaker that you keep for gluten-free bread. If you use a deep fryer, make sure that the oil doesn't become contaminated with gluten by using it to fry food coated with regular bread crumbs or batter.

Condiments, such as preserves and mayonnaise, can become contaminated with gluten—if, for instance, a knife or spoon is used to spread jelly on regular bread and then is dipped back into the jar—so always use clean utensils and encourage other people in your home to do the same. Another idea is to use squeeze containers or purchase separate jars and label them clearly as gluten free.

Once you've created a gluten-free zone, make sure that everyone else who uses the kitchen understands the importance of keeping things separate.

MILLET PORRIDGE
WITH APRICOT PUREE

Gluten-free millet makes a good replacement for oats, and the significant apricot content will boost your iron intake for the day.

SERVES: 4
PREP: 5 MINS COOK: 25 MINS

2¼ cups millet flakes
2 cups milk
pinch of salt
freshly grated nutmeg, to serve

APRICOT PUREE
¾ cup coarsely chopped dried apricots
1¼ cups water

1. To make the apricot puree, put the apricots into a saucepan and cover with the water. Bring to a boil, then reduce the heat and simmer, half covered, for 20 minutes, until the apricots are tender. Use a handheld blender or transfer the apricots, along with any water left in the saucepan, to a food processor or blender and process until smooth. Set aside.

2. To make the porridge, put the millet flakes into a saucepan and add the milk and salt. Bring to a boil, then reduce the heat and simmer for 5 minutes, stirring frequently, until cooked and creamy.

3. To serve, spoon into four bowls and top with the apricot puree and nutmeg.

APRICOT PUREE
Use plump, soft apricots to create a smooth and luxurious fruit puree.

PER SERVING: 289 CAL | 3G FAT | 1G SAT FAT | 52G CARBS | 12G SUGARS | 2.5G FIBER | 4.5G PROTEIN | 240MG SODIUM

PEAR, OAT, AND BLUEBERRY BREAKFAST LOAF

Blueberries and pears are a powerful combination, with blueberries full of antioxidants and pears with significant fiber as well as vitamins C and K.

MAKES: 1
PREP: 30 MINS COOK: 55 MINS–1 HOUR

1 cup sugar
7 tablespoons butter, plus extra for greasing
2 extra-large eggs, beaten
½ teaspoon vanilla extract
1 cup gluten-free all-purpose flour, sifted
1 teaspoon gluten-free baking powder
½ teaspoon gluten-free baking soda
¼ teaspoon xanthan gum
1 cup gluten-free oats,
plus extra for sprinkling
pinch of salt
½ teaspoon ground cinnamon
3 bananas, mashed
¼ cup milk
2 cooked or canned pear halves, diced
½ cup blueberries
1 tablespoon raw brown sugar, for sprinkling

1. Preheat the oven to 350°F. Grease a 9 x 5 x 3-inch loaf pan and line with parchment paper.

2. Cream the sugar and butter in a bowl. Add the eggs and vanilla extract slowly.

3. In a separate bowl, mix together the flour, baking powder, baking soda, xanthan gum, oats, salt, and cinnamon, then add to the egg mixture. Add the mashed banana and milk and mix well until combined.

4. Spoon half of the batter into the prepared loaf pan, then sprinkle with the diced pear and two-thirds of the blueberries. Spoon the remaining batter on top. Sprinkle with the remaining blueberries, the oats, and the raw sugar.

5. Bake in the preheated oven for 55 minutes–1 hour, or until a toothpick inserted in the center comes out clean. Remove from the oven and let cool in the pan.

NATURAL THICKENER
Xanthan gum is a natural product grown from the fermentation of the plant bacteria *Xanthomonas campestris*. It is used as a thickener to bind gluten-free bread and baked goods.

PER LOAF: 2,967 CAL | 110G FAT | 61G SAT FAT | 44G CARBS | 2,84G SUGARS | 15G FIBER | 40G PROTEIN | 2,680MG SODIUM

APRICOT AND RAISIN OAT BARS

There's no need to stick to traditional breakfast formats—these oat bars, combining natural sugars and gluten-free oats, offer the perfect simple start to the day.

MAKES: 12

PREP: 25 MINS, PLUS COOLING   COOK: 45–50 MINS

2 cups dried apricots
2 tablespoons sunflower oil, plus extra for oiling
finely grated zest of ½ orange
seeds from 5 cardamom pods, crushed (optional)
1 cup raisins
1¼ cups gluten–free rolled oats

1. Put the apricots into a saucepan with enough water to cover. Cook over medium heat until almost boiling, then reduce the heat and simmer for 5 minutes, or until completely soft. Drain.

2. Put the apricots into a food processor with the 2 tablespoons of oil and puree.

3. Transfer the puree to a bowl and stir in the orange zest and the cardamom seeds, if using. Let cool.

4. Preheat the oven to 350°F. Brush an 8–inch square baking pan with oil.

5. Stir the raisins and oats into the apricot mixture. Spread out in the prepared pan, leveling the surface with a spatula.

6. Bake in the preheated oven for 35–40 minutes, until firm. Cover with aluminum foil after about 25 minutes to prevent burning.

7. Let cool in the pan for 15 minutes. Turn out onto a wire rack and let cool completely before cutting into the bars.

MORNING SUSTENANCE
The oats in this breakfast bar help to make this a filling start to the day.

PER SERVING: 162 CAL | 3.1G FAT | 0.4G SAT FAT | 34.1G CARBS | 22.7G SUGARS | 3.6G FIBER | 2.6G PROTEIN | TRACE SODIUM

MUSHROOM HASH BROWNS

This is truly satisfying breakfast fare. The hash browns can also be prepared as a vegetarian main meal or as a snack served with yogurt or crème fraîche.

SERVES: 4
PREP: 25 MINS   COOK: 20–25 MINS

½ head celeriac, peeled
1 small onion
3 tablespoons chopped fresh parsley
4 portobello mushrooms
¼ cup olive oil
4 eggs
2 tablespoons milk
salt and pepper (optional)

1. Preheat the oven to 400°F. Coarsely grate the celeriac and onion in a food processor or by hand. Add 2 tablespoons of the parsley and season well.

2. Place the mushrooms on a baking sheet, brush with about 1 tablespoon of oil, and season with salt and pepper, if using. Bake for 10–12 minutes.

3. Heat 2 tablespoons of the oil in a large, heavy skillet. Place four large spoonfuls of the celeriac mixture in the pan, pressing with a spatula to flatten. Cook for about 10 minutes, turning once, until golden. Drain on paper towels and keep hot.

4. Meanwhile, beat the eggs with the milk, remaining parsley, and salt and pepper, if using. Heat the remaining oil in a small pan and cook the egg, stirring, until just set.

5. Place the hash browns on warm serving plates, top each with a mushroom, and spoon the scrambled eggs on top.

CELERIAC RECHARGE

Celeriac is low in calories and its flesh is full of healthy plant nutrients, minerals, vitamins, and fiber. It is also a rich source of vitamin K.

PER SERVING: 218 CAL | 17G FAT | 3G SAT FAT | 3.5G CARBS | 3G SUGARS | 5G FIBER | 10G PROTEIN | 160MG SODIUM

Gluten Free

BROCCOLI HASH

This version of hash features a mixture of healthy vegetables—broccoli, red bell pepper, and potatoes—and a touch of chile, creating a breakfast to remember.

SERVES: 4
PREP: 15 MINS COOK: 25 MINS

4 Yukon gold potatoes, cut into $1/2$-inch cubes
$2\frac{1}{2}$ cups small broccoli florets
2 tablespoons sunflower oil
1 onion, finely chopped
1 large red bell pepper, cut into small dice
$1/4$–$1/2$ teaspoon dried crushed red pepper flakes
4 extra-large eggs
salt and pepper (optional)

1. Cook the potatoes in lightly salted boiling water for 6 minutes. Drain well. Blanch or steam the broccoli for 3 minutes.

2. Heat the oil in a large skillet over medium-high heat, add the onion and red bell pepper, and sauté for 2–3 minutes to soften. Add the potatoes and cook, turning occasionally, for 6–8 minutes, until tender.

3. Stir in the broccoli and crushed red pepper flakes, then reduce the heat to low and cook, turning the mixture occasionally, until golden brown. Add salt and pepper, if using.

4. Meanwhile, bring a wide saucepan of water to just simmering point. Break the eggs into the water and poach gently for 3–4 minutes, until softly set.

5. Spoon the hash onto warm plates and top each portion with a poached egg.

EXCELLENT BROCCOLI
This versatile vegetable offers a rich supply of vitamins K and C, and is also a good source of folic acid, potassium, and fiber.

PER SERVING: 275 CAL | 12G FAT | 2.5G SAT FAT | 25G CARBS | 6G SUGARS | GG FIBER | 13.5G PROTEIN | 120MG SODIUM

Gluten Free

THREE-BEAN
ENERGY-BOOSTER SALAD

This mighty salad will give you a slow, sustained energy boost. It is made with low-GI foods that are rich in fiber and carbohydrate.

SERVES: 4
PREP: 20 MINS COOK: 8–10 MINS

2 cups halved green beans
1⅓ cups frozen edamame (soybeans)
or frozen fava beans
1 cup frozen corn kernels
1½ cups drained and rinsed, canned red kidney beans
2 tablespoons chia seeds

DRESSING
3 tablespoons olive oil
1 tablespoon red wine vinegar
1 teaspoon whole-grain mustard
1 teaspoon agave syrup
4 teaspoons finely chopped fresh tarragon
salt and pepper, to taste (optional)

1. Put the green beans, edamame, and corn kernels into a saucepan of boiling water. Bring back to a boil, then simmer for 4 minutes, until the green beans are just tender. Drain into a colander, rinse with cold water, then drain again and put into a salad bowl.

2. Add the kidney beans and chia seeds to the bowl and toss gently together.

3. To make the dressing, put the oil, vinegar, and mustard into a screw-top jar, then add the agave syrup and tarragon and season with salt and pepper, if using. Screw on the lid and shake well. Drizzle it over the salad, toss gently together, and serve immediately.

THREE CHEERS FOR CHIA
Originally eaten by the Mayans and Aztecs, chia seeds are rich in protein, which helps to build and repair muscles. They are the richest combined plant source of omega-3, –6, and –9 fatty acids. A tablespoon of chia seeds provides 5 grams of fiber; women should aim for 25 grams of fiber per day and men 38 grams.

PER SERVING: 312 CAL | 14.5G FAT | 2G SAT FAT | 26G CARBS | 6.5G SUGARS | FIBER: 13G FIBER | 13.5G PROTEIN | 40MG SODIUM

Gluten Free

TURKEY, RICE, AND CRANBERRY SALAD

Here's how to enjoy the flavor of turkey in a salad. You could take it to a potluck dinner, or pack individual portions for a work lunch.

SERVES: 4
PREP: 25 MINS, PLUS COOLING COOK: 30 MINS

3/4 cup brown rice
1/4 cup wild rice
9 ounces raw turkey breast slices
1/4 cup dried cranberries
3 scallions, finely chopped
2 tomatoes, diced
1 small red bell pepper, halved, seeded, and cut into chunks
2 cups arugula
1 1/2 ounces wafer-thin, sliced lean ham, cut into strips
salt and pepper (optional)

DRESSING

1 1/2 tablespoons cranberry sauce
1 1/2 tablespoons sherry vinegar
finely grated zest and juice of 1 small lemon
1 tablespoon Dijon mustard

1. Put cold water into the bottom half of a steamer, bring to a boil, then add the brown rice and wild rice and bring back to a boil. Put the turkey in the top of the steamer in a single layer, season with salt and pepper, if using, then put it on the bottom of the steamer, cover, and steam for 15 minutes, or until the turkey is cooked; cut into the middle of a slice to check that the meat is no longer pink and that the juices are clear and piping hot. Remove the steamer top and cook the rice for an additional 5—10 minutes, or according to package directions, until tender.

2. Dice the turkey and put it in a bowl. Add the cranberries. Drain and rinse the rice, then add to the bowl.

3. To make the dressing, put the cranberry sauce into a small saucepan and place over low heat until just melted. Remove from the heat, then add the vinegar, lemon zest and juice, mustard, and a little salt and pepper, if using. Whisk together until smooth, then drizzle it over the salad and let cool.

4. Add the scallions, tomatoes, and red bell pepper to the salad. Toss gently together, then divide among four plates. Top with the arugula and ham and serve.

DID YOU KNOW?

Meat from turkeys that graze on natural pasture contains a little more fat, including some omega-3 fats, and more carotenes than meat from penned turkeys.

PER SERVING: 320 CAL | 3G FAT | 0.7G SAT FAT | 48G CARBS | 12.5G SUGARS | 4G FIBER | 23G PROTEIN | 240MG SODIUM

Gluten Free

CHICKEN AND AVOCADO TACOS

The introduction of gluten-free tacos has brought the goodness and softness of a great tasting tortilla to those avoiding gluten—in all other respects this is a classic.

SERVES: 4
PREP: 20–25 MINS COOK: 10–13 MINS

1 ripe avocado
²⁄₃ cup plain yogurt
2 tablespoons medium cornmeal
1 teaspoon chili powder
½ teaspoon dried thyme
1 pound 5 ounces boneless, skinless chicken breasts,
cut into thin strips
2 tablespoons sunflower oil
1 red onion, sliced
1 large red bell pepper, seeded and sliced
1 large green bell pepper, seeded and sliced
8 gluten-free taco shells
salt and pepper (optional)
½ teaspoon smoked paprika, to garnish

1. Halve the avocado, remove the pit, and scoop out the flesh, then puree in a blender with the yogurt. Season with salt and pepper, if using.

2. Mix together the cornmeal, chilli, and thyme with salt and pepper, if using, in a large bowl. Add the chicken and toss to coat evenly.

3. Heat the oil in a wok or large skillet and sauté the onion and bell peppers for 3–4 minutes to soften. Remove and keep hot.

4. Add the chicken and cook, stirring occasionally, for 5–6 minutes, until evenly browned. Return the vegetables to the pan and sauté for an additional 1–2 minutes.

5. Spoon the chicken mixture into the taco shells and top with a spoonful of the avocado mixture. Sprinkle with smoked paprika and serve.

DID YOU KNOW?
Chicken is a good source of vitamin B6 and phosphorus, and of protein, niacin, and selenium.

PER SERVING: 502 CAL | 22.5G FAT | 3.5G SAT FAT | 30G CARBS | 9G SUGARS | 5.5G FIBER | 42.5G PROTEIN | 160MG SODIUM

SPICED CHICKPEA FLOUR ROLLS

Making these delicate, lightly spiced chickpea flour rolls is almost like making an Indian-style pasta. Creating perfect-looking rolls may take some practice!

MAKES: 24
PREP: 30–35 MINS, PLUS STANDING COOK: 30 MINS

1 tablespoon vegetable or peanut oil, for oiling
1²/₃ cups chickpea (besan or garbanzo bean) flour, sifted
½ cup plain yogurt
2½ cups warm water
2 teaspoons salt
¼ teaspoon ground turmeric
2 teaspoons grated fresh ginger
2 garlic cloves, crushed
4 teaspoons green chili paste

TOPPING
⅓ cup vegetable or peanut oil
1 teaspoon sesame seeds
1 teaspoon black mustard seeds
¼ cup finely chopped fresh cilantro
2 tablespoons freshly grated coconut

1. Lightly brush four large baking sheets with oil and set them aside.

2. Put the chickpea flour, yogurt, and water into a heavy saucepan with the salt, turmeric, ginger, garlic, and chili paste. Whisk until smooth, then put over medium heat and continue to whisk constantly. When the batter starts to thicken (after 5–6 minutes), reduce the heat to low, cover, and cook for 4–5 minutes. Stir, replace the lid, and cook for an additional 2–3 minutes, or until thickened and smooth.

3. Remove from the heat and ladle the batter onto the prepared baking sheets, using a spatula to spread it as thinly as possible. The batter will start to set as it cools. Let stand for 5 minutes, then slice it lengthwise into 2-inch-wide strips. This quantity should make about 24 rolls.

4. Starting at one end of each strip, use the spatula to gently lift and roll (like a small jellyroll). Repeat until all the strips have been rolled. Transfer to a serving plate.

5. Meanwhile, make the topping. Heat the oil in a skillet and add the sesame seeds and mustard seeds. When the seeds start to pop, remove from the heat and drizzle the spiced oil over the rolls. Sprinkle with the cilantro and coconut. Serve warm or at room temperature.

PER SERVING: 79 CAL | 4.5G FAT | 0.8G SAT FAT | 6G CARBS | 0.6G SUGARS | 1G FIBER | 3G PROTEIN | 160MG SODIUM

Gluten Free

QUINOA AND BEET BURGERS

Here's a burger with a difference. It will bring a resonant shade of purple to your plate, but in true burger tradition, it still provides a tasty treat.

MAKES: 8
PREP: 35 MINS COOK: 1 HOUR 10 MINS

3–4 small beets, peeled and cubed
3/4 cup quinoa, rinsed
1 1/2 cups vegetable broth
1/2 small onion, grated
finely grated zest of 1/2 lemon
2 teaspoons cumin seeds
1/2 teaspoon salt
1/4 teaspoon pepper
1 extra-large egg white, lightly beaten
4 teaspoons quinoa flour, for dusting
1 tablespoon vegetable oil, for pan-frying
8 slices of gluten-free sourdough toast, to serve
5 1/2 cups peppery salad greens, to serve

WASABI BUTTER
1 1/2 teaspoons wasabi powder
3/4 teaspoon warm water
5 tablespoons butter, at room temperature

1. Cook the beets in a steamer for 1 hour.

2. Meanwhile, put the quinoa into a saucepan with the broth. Bring to a boil, then cover and simmer over low heat for 10 minutes. Remove from the heat, but keep the pan covered for an additional 10 minutes to let the grains swell. Fluff up with a fork and spread out on a baking sheet to dry.

3. To make the wasabi butter, mix together the wasabi powder and water. Mix with the butter and chill in the refrigerator.

4. Place the beets into a food processor and process until smooth. Transfer to a bowl and mix with the quinoa, onion, lemon zest, cumin seeds, salt, pepper, and egg white.

5. Divide the mixture into eight equal portions and shape into patties, each 5/8 inch thick, firmly pressing the mixture together. Lightly dust with quinoa flour.

6. Heat the oil in a nonstick skillet. Add the patties and cook over medium-high heat, in batches if necessary, for 2 minutes on each side, turning carefully.

7. Place the burgers on the toast and serve with the wasabi butter and salad greens.

PER SERVING: 281 CAL | 11G FAT | 5G SAT FAT | 35G CARBS | 5G SUGARS | 4G FIBER | 9G PROTEIN | 520MG SODIUM

Gluten Free

BUCKWHEAT, MUSHROOMS, AND ROASTED SQUASH

Roasted buckwheat (or kasha) combined with mushrooms, onions, and balsamic-glazed squash provides this dish with appetizingly rich flavors.

SERVES: 4
PREP: 25 MINS COOK: 30 MINS

2¼ pounds winter squash, such as kabocha, buttercup, or butternut
1 tablespoon gluten-free thick balsamic vinegar
½ cup olive oil
large pat of butter
1⅓ cups roasted buckwheat, rinsed
1 egg, lightly beaten
2 cups hot gluten-free vegetable broth
½ teaspoon salt
1 onion, halved and sliced
4 cups quartered small cremini mushrooms
2 tablespoons lemon juice
⅓ cup chopped fresh flat-leaf parsley
¼ cup coarsely chopped walnut
additional salt and pepper (optional)

1. Preheat the oven to 400°F. Cut the squash into eight wedges, peel, and seed.

2. Put the squash into a roasting pan and toss with the vinegar and 6 tablespoons of the oil. Season well with salt and pepper, if using, and dot with the butter. Roast in the preheated oven for 25–30 minutes, until slightly caramelized.

3. Meanwhile, put the buckwheat into a skillet. Add the egg, stirring to coat the grains. Stir over medium heat for 3 minutes, until the egg moisture has evaporated. Add the broth and ½ teaspoon of salt. Simmer for 9–10 minutes, until the grains are tender but not disintegrating. Remove from the heat.

4. Heat the remaining oil in a deep skillet. Add the onion and sauté over medium heat for 10 minutes. Season with salt and pepper, if using. Add the mushrooms and sauté for 5 minutes. Stir in the buckwheat, lemon juice, and most of the parsley.

5. Transfer the buckwheat mixture to four plates and arrange the squash on top. Sprinkle with the walnuts and the remaining parsley. Serve.

PER SERVING: 655 CAL | 33G FAT | 6G SAT FAT | 70G CARBS | 15G SUGARS | 10G FIBER | 13.5G PROTEIN | 360MG SODIUM

Gluten Free

SPICED PARSNIP GRATIN
WITH GINGER CREAM

Can you imagine a gratin with no potatoes? Well, here it is—earthy, sweet parsnips are the key ingredient, providing an inventive spin on the classic gratin.

SERVES: 6 PREP: 20 MINS
COOK: 45–50 MINS

butter, for greasing
3 large parsnips (about 1 pound 10 ounces),
thinly sliced
2 cups heavy cream
1 cup gluten-free vegetable broth
1 garlic clove, crushed
1-inch piece fresh ginger, coarsely chopped
and crushed in a garlic press
¼ teaspoon white pepper
⅛ teaspoon freshly grated nutmeg,
plus extra to garnish
sea salt (optional)
snipped fresh chives, to garnish

1. Lightly grease a large gratin dish. Put the parsnips into a steamer set over a saucepan of boiling water. Steam for 3 minutes, until barely tender, shaking halfway through cooking. Transfer to the prepared dish and lightly season with salt, if using.

2. Preheat the oven to 350°F. Gently heat the cream and broth in a saucepan with the garlic and ginger. Do not let the mixture boil. Add the pepper, nutmeg, and sea salt, if using.

3. Pour the hot cream mixture over the parsnips. Cover the dish with aluminum foil and bake in the preheated oven for 20 minutes, with an oven pan underneath to catch any drips.

4. Remove the foil and bake for an additional 15–20 minutes, until golden on top.

5. Sprinkle with a little more nutmeg and some chives and serve.

DID YOU KNOW?
Parsnips are related to carrots and are ideal to grow into the winter, when frosts give the root a superior flavor. In Roman times, parsnips were thought to be an aphrodisiac.

PER SERVING: 456 CAL | 40G FAT | 24G SAT FAT | 1G CARBS | 8G SUGARS | 6G FIBER | 3.3G PROTEIN | 120MG SODIUM

SHRIMP JAMBALAYA

Jambalaya, a traditional Creole dish from New Orleans, has various guises, with the main ingredient varying from chicken and crayfish to shrimp and ham.

SERVES: 10
PREP: 25 MINS COOK: 35–45 MINS

2 tablespoons vegetable oil
2 onions, coarsely chopped
1 green bell pepper, seeded and coarsely chopped
2 celery stalks, coarsely chopped
3 garlic cloves, finely chopped
2 teaspoons paprika
10½ ounces skinless, boneless chicken breasts, chopped
3½ ounces gluten-free sausages, chopped
3 tomatoes, peeled and chopped
2⅓ cups long-grain rice
3¾ cups gluten-free chicken broth or fish broth
1 teaspoon dried oregano
2 bay leaves
12 large shrimp, peeled and deveined
4 scallions, finely chopped
salt and pepper (optional)
2 tablespoons chopped fresh flat-leaf parsley, to garnish

1. Heat the oil in a large skillet over low heat. Add the onions, green bell pepper, celery, and garlic and cook for 8–10 minutes, until all the vegetables have softened.

2. Stir in the paprika and cook for an additional 30 seconds. Add the chicken and sausages and cook for 8–10 minutes, or until lightly browned. Add the tomatoes and cook for 2–3 minutes, or until they have collapsed.

3. Add the rice to the pan and stir well. Pour in the broth, then add the oregano and bay leaves and stir well. Cover and simmer for 10 minutes.

4. Add the shrimp and stir. Replace the lid and cook for an additional 6–8 minutes, or according to package directions, until the rice is tender and the chicken and shrimp are cooked through.

5. Stir in the scallions and season with salt and pepper, if using. Remove and discard the bay leaves, garnish with parsley, and serve immediately.

POWER SHRIMP
Shrimp provide a rich source of high-quality protein, as well as a range of essential vitamins and minerals—such as iron, selenium, and zinc—for those following a healthy diet. They are also notably low in calories.

PER SERVING: 755 CAL | 16G FAT | 3.8G SAT FAT | 108G CARBS | 7.3G SUGARS | 5.6G FIBER | 43.2G PROTEIN | 1,960MG SODIUM

BARBECUE-GLAZED SPARERIBS

The best part of barbecue-glazed spareribs is the primeval joy of digging into them. Listed here as optional, a crisp green salad will add both color and texture.

SERVES: 4

PREP: 20 MINS COOK: 1¼ HOURS

2 racks pork spareribs, about 1³/4 pounds each
3 tablespoons instant coffee granules, dissolved in ¹/3 cup hot water
¹/3 cup gluten-free ketchup
2 tablespoons vegetable oil
3 tablespoons gluten-free Worcestershire sauce
3 tablespoons gluten-free mango chutney
salt and pepper (optional)
crisp green salad, to serve (optional)

1. Put the racks of ribs into a large saucepan and cover with water. Bring to a boil, skim off any scum from the surface, then simmer for 25 minutes.

2. Lift the ribs out of the water and place on a metal rack set over a large roasting pan. Preheat the oven to 375°F.

3. Put the coffee, ketchup, oil, Worcestershire sauce, and chutney into a bowl and mix together. Season with salt and pepper, if using.

4. Liberally brush the coffee glaze over the racks of ribs. Roast in the preheated oven for 45 minutes, basting occasionally, until the glaze is sticky and lightly charred in places and the ribs are tender.

5. Serve the glazed ribs immediately with salad on the side, if using.

PORK PROTEIN
Pork is a good source of protein and contains many other key nutrients—for example, it is high in potassium, zinc, and iron.

PER SERVING: 910 CAL | 66.8G FAT | 30.9G SAT FAT | 17.3G CARBS | 12.8G SUGARS | 0.4G FIBER | 66.6G PROTEIN | 1,280MG SODIUM

Gluten Free

BLUEBERRY AND LIME SAGO DESSERT

The small balls, or pearls, of sago are noteworthy for their very high carbohydrate, low-fiber content and are easy to digest.

SERVES: 4
PREP: 20–25 MINS, PLUS COOLING AND CHILLING
COOK: 35 MINS

1¼ cups coconut milk
1¼ cups water
½ cup sago or tapioca pearls
⅓ cup shredded coconut
⅓ cup sugar
grated zest and juice of 1 lime
1 teaspoon vanilla extract
½ teaspoon ground cinnamon
¼ teaspoon grated nutmeg
20 blueberries
⅓ cup diced fresh mango

1. Bring the coconut milk and water to a boil in a saucepan over medium heat. Pour in the sago, stirring with a fork to keep the pearls separate. Turn down the heat and simmer on low heat for 20 minutes, stirring frequently to prevent the sago from sticking to the pan.

2. Meanwhile, put the coconut into a nonstick skillet over high heat, stirring occasionally, for 1 minute, or until it turns golden. Immediately remove from the heat and set aside.

3. When the sago has simmered for 20 minutes, add the sugar, lime zest and half the juice, the vanilla extract, and spices. Stir well and simmer for an additional 10 minutes, or until the sago pearls are virtually transparent and tender. If the mixture becomes too thick to simmer before the sago is cooked through, add a little boiling water and mix in thoroughly. When the sago is ready, remove the pan from the heat and stir in the remaining lime juice. Let cool for 10 minutes.

4. Spoon the sago mixture into four stemmed glasses or ramekins (individual ceramic dishes) and smooth the top with the back of the spoon. Cover and chill for 30 minutes–1 hour. Decorate each dessert with one-quarter of the toasted coconut, blueberries, and diced mango.

PER SERVING: 280 CAL | 15G FAT | 13G SAT FAT | 33G CARBS | 15G SUGARS | 2G FIBER | 1.5G PROTEIN | TRACE SODIUM

Gluten Free

APPLE AND CINNAMON PIE

Simply perfect in fall or winter, this is a generous showstopper dessert to finish off any family meal or dinner party.

SERVES: 8
PREP: 35 MINS COOK: 30 MINS

PIE DOUGH
1/3 cup vegetable shortening
1 tablespoon gluten-free margarine
1 1/3 cups gluten-free all-purpose flour
1 tablespoon gluten-free baking powder
pinch of salt
4 teaspoons gluten-free all-purpose flour, for dusting
1 tablespoon gluten-free soy milk, for brushing
1 tablespoon sugar, for sprinkling

FILLING
6–7 cooking apples (about 2 1/4 pounds), such as Granny Smiths, peeled, cored, and sliced
3/4 cup sugar
2 teaspoons gluten-free cornstarch
1 tablespoon ground cinnamon

1. To make the dough, put the vegetable shortening and margarine into a large mixing bowl. Pour in 1/2 cup of boiling water and mix with a wooden spoon until creamy. Add the flour, baking powder, and salt, stir together, then turn out onto a lightly floured work surface and knead together into a smooth ball. Let the dough cool for 5 minutes. Roll the dough out on a sheet of plastic wrap to a shape that slightly overhangs a 9-inch round pie plate. Set aside.

2. Preheat the oven to 350°F.

3. Place the apples into a large saucepan with the sugar, cornstarch, and cinnamon, and add 3 tablespoons of water. Cook gently for 5–10 minutes, or until the apples are just tender and most of the liquid in the pan has been thickened by the cornstarch. Let the mixture cool.

4. Put the apple filling into the pie plate. Lift the dough on the sheet of plastic wrap (to support it) and carefully transfer the dough to the top of the pie, removing the plastic wrap and pressing the edges down to form a crust and trimming away any excess with a sharp knife. Reroll the scraps to make decorative leaves and place them on top of the pie.

5. Brush the top of the pie with a little soy milk and sprinkle with a little sugar. Bake in the preheated oven for 30 minutes, or until just golden. Serve hot or cold.

PER SERVING: 330 CAL | 10G FAT | 4G SAT FAT | 55G CARBS | 31G SUGARS | 4G FIBER | 3.5G PROTEIN | 200MG SODIUM

ANGEL FOOD CAKE

You'll feel light as a feather after a piece of this airy cake made with rice flour, tapioca flour, and gluten-free cornstarch.

MAKES: 1 CAKE
PREP: 15 MINS, PLUS STANDING
COOK: 45 MINS

butter, for greasing
10 egg whites
½ cup white rice flour
½ cup tapioca (cassava) flour
½ cup gluten-free cornstarch
⅓ cup potato flour
1½ cups superfine or granulated sugar
1½ teaspoons gluten-free cream of tartar
½ teaspoon vanilla extract
½ teaspoon salt
4⅓ cups frozen mixed berries (optional)
⅓ cup superfine or granulated sugar (optional)
4 teaspoons confectioners' sugar, to decorate

1. Preheat the oven to 350°F. Grease an 8-inch cake pan and line with parchment paper.

2. Let the egg whites sit for about 30 minutes at room temperature in a large bowl. In a separate bowl, sift the white rice flour, tapioca flour, cornstarch, potato flour, and ¾ cup of the sugar.

3. Using a food processor or mixer, whisk the egg whites with the cream of tartar, vanilla extract, and salt until soft peaks form. Gradually add the remaining ¾ cup of sugar until stiff peaks develop. Add the flour mixture and fold in.

4. Spoon the batter into the prepared pan and bake in the preheated oven for about 45 minutes, until firm to the touch and a toothpick inserted in the center comes out clean.

5. Remove from the oven and, keeping the cake in the pan, turn upside down to cool on a wire rack. Poach the fruits with the superfine or granulated sugar gently until soft, if using. Let cool completely. When the cake is cool, remove from the pan and decorate with confectioners' sugar and the drained mixed fruit, if desired.

TURN TO TAPIOCA
Tapioca, or cassava, flour is a starchy white flour with a gentle, sweet flavor. It is used as an alternative to traditional wheat flours.

PER CAKE: 2,784 CAL | 7G FAT | 3G SAT FAT | 618G CARBS | 419G SUGARS | 25G FIBER | 50G PROTEIN | 1,640MG SODIUM

PISTACHIO MACARONS

A delicious gluten-free option, pistachios are a good source of fiber and protein and can help to lower cholesterol and prevent cardiovascular disease.

MAKES: 24
PREP: 25 MINS, PLUS COOLING COOK: 20 MINS

⅓ cup skinned pistachio nuts, plus extra
to decorate
⅓ cup confectioners' sugar
1 tablespoon rice flour
2 egg whites
¼ cup superfine sugar
¾ cup dry unsweeten coconut
1 tablespoon chopped fresh mint

1. Preheat the oven to 350°F. Line two baking sheets with parchment paper.

2. Put the pistachio nuts, confectioners' sugar, and rice flour into a food processor and process until finely ground.

3. Whisk the egg whites in a clean, dry bowl until stiff, then gradually whisk in the superfine sugar. Fold in the pistachio mixture, coconut, and mint.

4. Place spoonfuls of the paste onto the prepared baking sheets and press a pistachio on top of each to decorate.

5. Bake in the preheated oven for about 20 minutes, until firm and just beginning to brown. Cool on the baking sheet and serve.

DID YOU KNOW?
Pistachios—originally from Turkey and the Middle East—get their green color from chlorophyll, the same chemical found in leaves. It's this that makes pistachios such a good source of carotenes.

PER SERVING: 37 CAL | 2.5G FAT | 1.5G SAT FAT | 2.5G CARBS | 2G SUGARS | 0.4G FIBER | 1G PROTEIN | TRACE SODIUM

VEGAN

WHAT DOES IT MEAN TO BE A VEGAN?

Being vegan means not using any products that come from animals. It's not always just a dietary choice either; it is often also a lifestyle choice. Strict vegans avoid all animal products when choosing clothing, toiletries, medicine, and cleaning products, as well as in their general diet.

PEOPLE GO VEGAN FOR MANY REASONS, BUT THE MOST COMMON ARE:

- Because they don't want to support practices that they believe are cruel to animals

- Because they don't want to support practices that they believe are damaging to the environment

- Because they believe that it would be easier to feed the world's population if more people were vegan

- Because they believe that it is good for their health.

Of course, it's perfectly possible to be a "junk food vegan" and live on highly processed meat substitutes and vegan cupcakes piled high with colorful frosting. But most vegans respect their own health and many make other health-related changes to their diets by, for instance, avoiding alcohol, sugar, and caffeine.

A well-balanced, plant-base diet has many health benefits. You'll probably find yourself consuming less fat, especially less saturated fat and cholesterol. Fruit and vegetables are naturally high in fiber, and are good sources of vitamins A and C, while whole grains and nuts are good sources of the B vitamins and vitamin E. Plant foods are also rich in antioxidants and phytochemicals, which are believed to protect against some diseases, including certain cancers. A lot of vegans believe that a good, balanced vegan diet is beneficial to their overall health.

In the following pages, you'll find much more information about the steps you can take to make sure your vegan diet is good for you. You'll also find inspiring meal options that will prove you can eat exciting vegan-friendly food any time of the day. Keeping your diet varied is key to enjoying a vegan lifestyle, and this book provides a lot of options for meals and snacks.

This chapter offers recipes for a variety of delicious dishes that everybody, including nonvegans, will enjoy. Vegetarians and meat eaters will be surprised by how tasty some of these dishes are, so these meals are also good for entertaining a range of guests.

WHAT SHOULD YOU EAT TO BE A HEALTHY VEGAN?

The best way to maintain good health is to consume plenty of fresh fruit and vegetables, whole grains, beans, nuts, and seeds. These are key parts of a vegan diet, so make sure to keep a good mixture in your day-to-day diet. Trying new foods and eating a variety of dishes will help to make sure that your body doesn't run low on anything it needs.

VITAMINS

There is only one important nutrient missing from a 100-percent, plant-base diet, and that's vitamin B_{12}, which occurs naturally only in animal-derived products. In the long term, a diet lacking in vitamin B_{12} can cause irreversible damage to the nervous system, so it is important to monitor that you are taking on board enough of this vitamin.

The Vegan Society recommends that you take a B_{12} supplement and look for vegan foods that contain added vitamin B_{12}, such as yeast extracts, nutritional yeast flakes, breakfast cereals, and nondairy milks.

Apart from vitamin B_{12}, a diet based on fresh fruit and vegetables, legumes, nuts, seeds, and whole grains will provide a complete spectrum of vitamins. Good vegan sources of vitamin D include fortified margarines, nondairy milks, and breakfast cereals. It is essential to eat a good variety of food to make sure you are getting all your vitamins instead of sticking to the same favorite meals.

MINERALS

A vegan diet includes a wide range of foods that are good sources of iron, including dark green leafy vegetables, beans, and soy products. Consuming vitamin C at the same time helps our bodies to absorb iron—and many vegan foods contain iron and vitamin C together. It is also a good idea to drink a vitamin-C rich juice alongside a main meal to be sure that you consume vitamin C and iron together.

Iodine plays a part in thyroid regulation, and it's especially important if you're pregnant, because deficiency can harm your baby's brain development.

In the typical American diet, the main source of iodine is milk—vegans obtain iodine from cereal products, sea salt, and seaweeds, such as nori and kombu.

GOOD FATS

A vegan diet is naturally low in saturated fats and cholesterol. But we need to make sure that we still consume "good fats" to get all the essential fatty acids that our bodies can't make on their own. Omega 6 is plentiful in a vegan diet, but unfortunately the most commonly recommended source of Omega 3 is fish oil.

The best vegan sources of Omega 3 are cold-pressed seed oils, such as flaxseed, hemp seed, and canola oil, along with chia seeds, walnuts, and Brazil nuts. These oils, seeds, and nuts are available from most health food stores.

Vegan Omega 3 supplements are often made with marine algae. Some nondairy milks are fortified with vegan-friendly Omega 3 oils. When buying any supplements, it is worth checking the package to make sure that the oils are not provided in gelatin-like capsules or lozenges that are made from the animal product gelatin.

CARBS AND FIBER

Omitting meat, dairy products, and eggs from your diet has no negative effect on your consumption of fiber or carbohydrates; in fact, a vegan diet will probably contain more of these essential macronutrients, because there is a lot of fiber in beans, fruit, and vegetables. As long as you make sure that you are eating a good range of these ingredients, your carbohydrate and fiber levels should be fine.

Whole-grain cereal products are a good choice for breakfast, not just because they contain more fiber than their white counterparts, but because the energy they contain is released gradually. This will give you more energy during the course of the day.

PROTEIN

Meat and eggs are called "complete proteins," because they contain all the amino acids your body needs. Most plant foods don't contain all the essential amino acids, so you should aim to eat a variety of vegan protein sources including nuts, seeds, grains, and legumes. The notable exceptions are quinoa and soy—both of these plant foods are complete proteins. Tofu, in particular, is a food that is well worth investigating, and although it can seem uninspiring when it's fresh from the package, a little culinary know-how can transform it into a nutritious favorite. Marinating or braising tofu can perform wonders and turn this simple ingredient into something really tasty and versatile.

HOW TO STOCK YOUR FOOD PANTRY

Knowing how to stock a vegan-friendly food pantry is a great way to keep organized in the kitchen. Locating a good whole-food store in your area can be a revelation, but you can always find everything you need online. Most supermarkets are also now getting better at stocking vegan-friendly foods, with a lot of ordinary supermarkets now stocking a range of nondairy milks and margarines.

Make smart purchases by selecting products such as soy milks, breakfast cereals, and snack bars that contain added nutrients. Make sure your pantry includes foods that are fortified with vitamin B_{12}, such as yeast extracts and nutritional yeast flakes.

FOODS TO CHECK

Vegan shoppers soon become used to reading the small print on food labels. As a shortcut, a quick look at the allergy advice on food labels should indicate whether they contain eggs or dairy products, because these are common allergens.

GELATIN

Made from animal by-products, gelatin is used in a lot of low-fat foods, especially desserts and candies, but also appears in margarines and breakfast cereals. It's also used to make the capsules for many health supplements.

LACTOSE

This is a form of sugar derived from milk. Look for it in gravy and bouillon powders, and in snacks, such as potato chips, where it is used as a flavor carrier.

SUGAR

White sugar from sugarcane is sometimes whitened using a process that requires charcoal made with animal bones. White beet sugar is not subject to this process. If in doubt, choose brown sugar or try a substitute. Check any prepared products that may contain sugar to make sure they are vegan-friendly.

COCHINEAL

This red food coloring is made from crushed beetles.

WHEY

This by-product of the cheese-making process is never vegan, and may not even be vegetarian if animal rennet has been used to separate the milk into curds and whey.

PASTRY

This is often made with butter and sometimes made with lard. Glazed pastries have probably been brushed with milk or egg.

"-FREE" FOODS

Don't assume that any of the items that are labeled as dairy-free or gluten-free, for example, are also vegan. They might be free from dairy or eggs, but not both, and gluten-free products often rely on eggs to hold them together. Likewise, vegetarian products can be vegan, but they can also contain dairy or eggs.

WAX

Several kinds of wax can be used to enhance the shine and shelf life of fruit and vegetables. Some waxes are made from paraffin or petroleum, but others may contain nonvegan animal-base products, such as shellac. At present, most food labeling doesn't give these details.

Look for produce that is seasonal and grown locally, because it probably won't have wax added as a preservative to help it travel long distances. There are vegetable-washing products available, but if in doubt, ask the store's Customer Services and Technical Department and peel your purchases.

SPICED QUINOA BREAKFAST BOWL WITH PECANS

Quinoa is packed with protein, making it a fantastic grain to include in a healthy breakfast. Here, it's combined with zingy spices, sweet pears, and crunchy nuts for a breakfast that's worth getting out of bed for.

SERVES: 2
PREP: 15 MINS COOK: 15 MINS

⅓ cup uncooked quinoa, rinsed well
⅔ cup water
¼ teaspoon ground cinnamon
¼ teaspoon ground nutmeg
¼ teaspoon ground allspice
pinch of salt
4 teaspoons maple syrup
½ cup almond milk
1 pear, cored and diced
¼ cup pecans, toasted

1. In a small saucepan, combine the quinoa with the water, cinnamon, nutmeg, allspice, and salt and bring to a boil over medium-high heat. Reduce the heat to low, cover, and simmer for about 15 minutes, until the quinoa is tender.

2. Stir in the maple syrup and divide the mixture between two serving bowls. Pour the almond milk over the top, dividing equally, and top with the pear pieces and pecans. Serve immediately.

GOLDEN QUINOA
Quinoa is native to Peru and Bolivia, where it was known as "the golden grain" of the Incas. It is said to be the only plant food that contains all nine essential amino acids, putting it on a par with animal protein.

PER SERVING: 320 CALS | 15.5G FAT | 1.4G SAT FAT | 42.9G CARBS | 17.3G SUGARS | 6.8G FIBER | 6.1G PROTEIN | 320MG SODIUM

Vegan

MUSHROOMS ON BRUSCHETTA

Nutritious mushrooms are star of this simple topped vegan baguette.
It can be cooked in a flash and is best enjoyed warm.

SERVES: 4
PREP: 15 MINS COOK: 10 MINS

12 slices vegan baguette, each
½ inch thick
3 tablespoons olive oil
2 garlic cloves, crushed
3⅔ cups sliced cremini mushrooms
8 ounces mixed wild mushrooms
2 teaspoons lemon juice
2 tablespoons chopped fresh flat-leaf parsley
salt and pepper (optional)

1. Place the slices of baguette on a ridged grill pan and toast on both sides until golden. Reserve and keep warm.

2. Meanwhile, heat the oil in a skillet. Add the garlic and cook gently for a few seconds, then add the cremini mushrooms. Cook, stirring constantly, over high heat for 3 minutes. Add the wild mushrooms and cook for an additional 2 minutes. Stir in the lemon juice.

3. Season with salt and pepper, if using, and stir in the chopped parsley.

4. Spoon the mushroom mixture onto the warm toast and serve immediately.

MIGHTY MUSHROOMS
The compounds in mushrooms, which help boost the immune system, help to prevent cancers, infections, and autoimmune diseases.

PER SERVING: 327 CALS | 12.3G FAT | 1.8G SAT FAT | 45.1G CARBS | 4.9G SUGARS | 3.6G FIBER | 11.3G PROTEIN | 440MG SODIUM

HOMEMADE CACAO AND HAZELNUT BUTTER

This healthy hazelnut butter is delicious for breakfast, plus it keeps well for several days.

MAKES: ABOUT 1 CUP
PREP: 15 MINS, PLUS STANDING COOK: 3–4 MINS

3/4 cup unblanched hazelnuts
1/4 cup raw cacao powder
1/3 cup firmly packed light brown sugar
1/2 cup light olive oil
1/2 teaspoon vanilla extract
pinch of salt

1. Add the hazelnuts to a dry skillet and cook over medium heat for 3–4 minutes, constantly shaking the pan, until the nuts are an even golden brown.

2. Wrap the nuts in a clean dish towel and rub the outsides to remove the skins.

3. Put the nuts into a blender and blend until finely ground. Add the cacao powder, sugar, oil, vanilla extract, and salt, then blend again to make a smooth paste.

4. Spoon into a small airtight jar and secure the lid. Let stand at room temperature for 4 hours, until the sugar has dissolved completely. Stir again, then store in the refrigerator for up to five days.

SUITS YOU
This can be served many ways but it is really delicious spread on tasty vegan whole-grain toast.

PER 45G SERVING: 430 CALS | 40G FAT | 5.2G SAT FAT | 19.5G CARBS | 13.9G SUGARS | 4G FIBER | 4.1G PROTEIN | 120MG SODIUM

BANANA FLATBREAD BITES
WITH TAHINI AND DATE SYRUP

Sometimes the best things are the simplest. Assembled in minutes, this speedy breakfast is perfect for a busy morning.

SERVES: 4
PREP: 15 MINS COOK: 5–6 MINS

4 (8–inch) vegan whole–wheat tortillas
¼ cup tahini
3 tablespoons date syrup
4 bananas, peeled

1. Preheat a dry skillet, then add the tortillas, one by one, and warm for 30 seconds on each side.

2. Arrange the tortillas on a cutting board, thinly spread each with 1 tablespoon of the tahini, then drizzle with the date syrup. Add a whole banana to each tortilla, just a little off–center, then roll up tightly.

3. Cut each tortilla into thick slices, secure the bites with a toothpick, and arrange on a plate. Serve warm.

GO BANANAS
Bananas are the only fruit to contain both tryptophan and vitamin B_6, which produce serotonin—the natural chemical that helps lift your mood.

PER SERVING: 354 CALS | 11.3G FAT | 2.5G SAT FAT | 60G CARBS | 25.4G SUGARS | 4.1G FIBER | 9.4G PROTEIN | 200MG SODIUM

KIWI QUENCHER

A combination to get you glowing from the inside out, jewel-like kiwi is blended with juicy green grapes and thirst-quenching lettuce.

SERVES: 1

PREP: 15 MINS COOK: NONE

½ romaine lettuce
4 kiwis, peeled
¾ cup green grapes
1 large pear, halved
handful of ice, to serve (optional)

1. Peel off a lettuce leaf and reserve. Feed the kiwis and grapes, lettuce, and pear through a juicer.

2. Fill a glass halfway with ice, if using, then pour in the juice.

3. Garnish with the reserved lettuce leaf and serve immediately.

SUPER KIWI

A single kiwi contains more immune-boosting vitamin C than the recommended daily allowance and as much potassium as a small banana.

PER SERVING: 431 CALS | 2.8G FAT | 0.3G SAT FAT | 106G CARBS | 68G SUGARS | 5G FIBER | 8.5G PROTEIN | 40MG SODIUM

Vegan

MASHED AVOCADO AND QUINOA WRAP

Filled with nourishing, natural nutrients, fresh avocado and spinach combine with colorful, crunchy raw red cabbage to create these really appealing quinoa-topped wraps. They are great for sharing, because everyone can assemble their own.

SERVES: 4

PREP: 20 MINS, PLUS COOLING   COOK: 15–18 MINS

1 cup quinoa, rinsed
1²/₃ cups vegan broth
1 large, ripe avocado, peeled and pitted
½ teaspoon smoked paprika
2 garlic cloves, crushed
grated zest and juice of 1 lemon
4 vegan whole-wheat tortillas
1³/₄ cups baby spinach
2 cups finely sliced red cabbage
salt and pepper (optional)

1. Put the quinoa and vegan broth into a small saucepan and simmer, covered, for 15–18 minutes, or until the broth has been completely absorbed. Set aside to cool.

2. Meanwhile, gently mash the avocado flesh with the smoked paprika, crushed garlic, lemon zest, and just enough lemon juice to make a thick consistency.

3. Spread the mashed avocado down the center of each wrap and then top with the warm quinoa, spinach, and red cabbage. Season with salt and pepper, if using. Tuck in the ends and tightly fold or roll into a wrap and serve immediately.

RED CABBAGE FOR HEALTH

Red cabbage is rich in compounds that help to protect us from cancers and the signs of aging. It is also higher in vitamin C than pale varieties and is a good source of minerals, including calcium and selenium.

PER SERVING: 385 CALS | 13.2G FAT | 2.8G SAT FAT | 56.8G CARBS | 3.6G SUGARS | 10.4G FIBER | 11.8G PROTEIN | 560MG SODIUM

BARLEY AND CRUSHED BEAN SALAD

Tossed with summery vegetables, pearl barley makes a filling salad. It's packed with complex carbs and soluble fiber and is a low-GI food.

SERVES: 4
PREP: 10–15 MINS COOK: 25–30 MINS

5 cups vegan broth
3/4 cup pearl barley
1 cup shelled fava beans
(about 4 cups in the pods)
1 cup peas
2 scallions, quartered
2 stems of fresh tarragon, finely chopped
1/2 cup finely chopped fresh flat–leaf parsley
1/3 cup pea shoots

DRESSING

2 tablespoons flaxseed oil
2 tablespoons rice bran oil
1 tablespoon vegan white wine vinegar
1 teaspoon vegan Dijon mustard
1 teaspoon coriander seeds, coarsely crushed
1/4 teaspoon crushed red pepper flakes
pepper (optional)

1. Put the broth into the bottom of a steamer, bring to a boil, then add the pearl barley, cover, and simmer for 20 minutes, or according to package directions, subtracting 5–10 minutes. Put the fava beans in the top of the steamer, then put it on the bottom half of the steamer, cover, and steam for 5–10 minutes, or until the barley and beans are just tender.

2. Drain off the broth and discard, then spoon the barley into a salad bowl. Add one–third of the fava beans and raw peas. Put the remaining fava beans and peas, the scallions, tarragon, and parsley into a food processor and process until finely chopped. Add to the salad bowl.

3. To make the dressing, put the flaxseed oil, rice bran oil, vinegar, mustard, coriander seeds, and red pepper flakes into a screw–top jar, season with pepper, if using, screw on the lid, and shake well. Drizzle the dressing over the salad and toss gently together, then spoon into four bowls, top with the pea shoots, and serve.

PROTEIN BOOSTERS

Proteins are an essential constituent of virtually every cell in the body; in fact, the word comes from the Greek meaning "of prime importance." They are needed for growth and repair of body tissues, to make up enzymes and hormones, and as neurotransmitters. Unlike meat, most vegetable proteins do not contain all nine essential amino acids, so aim to mix different vegetable proteins together in one meal by serving grains and legumes together.

PER SERVING: 265 CALS | 15.7G FAT | 3.3G SAT FAT | 22.7G CARBS | 3.6G SUGARS | 5.9G FIBER | 7G PROTEIN | 1,160MG SODIUM

SPICY PEANUT SOUP

This spicy and satisfying soup gets rich flavor from peanut butter and a kick from herbs and chiles. Serve it with hunks of crusty bread for dunking or over steamed rice.

SERVES: 4

PREP: 15 MINS   COOK: 35–40 MINS

1 tablespoon vegetable oil
1 small onion, chopped
1 tablespoon finely chopped fresh ginger
2 garlic cloves, finely chopped
1/2 teaspoon ground cumin
1/4 teaspoon pepper
1/4 teaspoon ground cinnamon
1/4 teaspoon cayenne pepper
1/4 teaspoon turmeric
1 1/2 teaspoons salt
3 serrano chiles, finely chopped
2 2/3 cups peeled and diced sweet potatoes
3 cups vegan broth
1 2/3 cups canned diced tomatoes, with their can juices
1/2 cup unsweetened peanut butter
1/2 cup coconut milk
juice of 1 lemon
2 tablespoons chopped fresh cilantro leaves
2 scallions, thinly sliced, and chopped fresh cilantro sprigs, to garnish (optional)

1. Heat the oil in a medium saucepan over medium heat. Add the onion and cook, stirring frequently, for 10 minutes, until soft. Stir in the ginger, garlic, cumin, pepper, cinnamon, cayenne pepper, turmeric, and salt.

2. Add the chiles, sweet potatoes, and broth and increase the heat to medium–high. Bring the mixture to a boil, then reduce the heat to medium–low and simmer for 20 minutes, until the sweet potatoes are tender.

3. Add the tomatoes with their can juices and the peanut butter. Puree the soup in a blender. Return the soup to the pan and stir in the coconut milk, lemon juice, and cilantro. Heat over medium heat until heated through. Serve hot, garnished with the scallions and cilantro sprigs, if using.

GO NUTS
Peanuts are a great source of copper, an essential mineral for red blood cell formation and for building a healthy immune system, blood vessels, and bones.

PER SERVING: 402 CALS | 26.6G FAT | 9.2G SAT FAT | 34.9G CARBS | 13.3G SUGARS | 5.8G FIBER | 11.7G PROTEIN | 1,800MG SODIUM

APPLE AND CINNAMON CHIPS

Crisp and crunchy, without the fat, salt, and strong flavors of potato chips, these apple chips are a much healthier alternative for all the family.

SERVES: 4
PREP: 20–25 MINS, PLUS COOLING   COOK: 1½–2 HOURS

4 cups water
1 tablespoon salt
3 crisp, sweet apples, such as Braeburn or Gala
¼ teaspoon ground cinnamon

1. Preheat the oven to 225°F. Put the water and salt into a large mixing bowl and stir until the salt has dissolved.

2. Slice the apples thinly, one at a time, with a sharp knife or mandoline slicer, leaving the skin on and the core still in place, but removing any seeds. Add each apple slice to the water. Turn to coat in the salt water, which will help prevent discoloration.

3. Drain the apple slices in a colander, then lightly pat dry with a clean dish towel. Arrange in a thin layer on a large cooking or roasting rack. Put it into the oven so that the heat can circulate under the slices as well as over the tops.

4. Bake for 1½–2 hours, until the apple slices are dry and crisp. Loosen with a spatula and transfer to a large plate or cutting board, then sprinkle with cinnamon. Let cool completely, then serve.

KEEP COOL
Pack any leftovers into a plastic container, seal, and keep in the refrigerator for up to two days.

PER SERVING: 72 CALS | 0.2G FAT | TRACE SAT FAT | 19.1G CARBS | 14.2G SUGARS | 3.4G FIBER | 0.3G PROTEIN | 280MG SODIUM

Vegan

FIVE-SPICE
CASHEW NUTS

*Chinese five-spice powder is a popular seasoning mixture in Chinese cooking.
Made up of equal parts Sichuan peppercorns, star anise, fennel seeds,
cloves, and cinnamon, it is both sweet and spicy.*

SERVES: 8
PREP: 5 MINS, PLUS COOLING   COOK: 10–12 MINS

1 tablespoon peanut oil, for oiling
½ teaspoon Sichuan peppercorns
2 star anise pods
½ teaspoon fennel seeds
6 whole cloves
½ teaspoon ground cinnamon
2 tablespoons water
¼ cup firmly packed light brown sugar
1 teaspoon salt
2 cups unsalted cashew nuts

1. Preheat the oven to 400°F. Lightly oil a baking pan and a large piece of aluminum foil.

2. In a spice grinder, grind together the peppercorns, star anise pods, fennel seeds, and cloves until finely ground. Add the cinnamon and mix well.

3. Put the water and sugar into a medium saucepan and heat over medium heat, stirring constantly, for 2 minutes, or until the sugar is dissolved. Add the spice mixture and salt and stir to mix well. Add the nuts and stir to coat completely. Cook, stirring, for an additional minute.

4. Transfer the nuts to the prepared baking pan and spread out in an even layer. Roast in the preheated oven for 6–8 minutes, until most of the liquid has evaporated. Transfer the nuts to the prepared foil and separate them so that they don't stick together. Let cool completely before serving.

5. Store in an airtight container at room temperature for up to two weeks.

DID YOU KNOW?
Many supermarkets carry five–spice powder in the spice section. You can use 2½ teaspoons of the mix in this recipe instead of the Sichuan peppercorns, star anise, fennel seeds, cloves, and cinnamon.

PER SERVING: 219 CALS | 16.2G FAT | 3.2G SAT FAT | 16.6G CARBS | 7.6G SUGARS | 1.1G FIBER | 4.8G PROTEIN | 320MG SODIUM

Vegan

RED CURRY WITH MIXED GREENS

This dish does it all—it's ideal for a quick midweek meal but is impressive enough to serve to family and friends as well.

SERVES: 4
PREP: 15 MINS COOK: 20 MINS

2 tablespoons peanut oil
2 onions, thinly sliced
1 bunch of fine asparagus spears
1²/₃ cups coconut milk
2 tablespoons vegan red curry paste
3 fresh kaffir lime leaves
8 cups baby spinach leaves
2 small heads of bok choy, chopped
1 head of Chinese greens, shredded
¼ cup chopped fresh cilantro

1. Heat a wok over medium-high heat and add the oil. Add the onions and asparagus and stir-fry for 1–2 minutes.

2. Add the coconut milk, curry paste, and lime leaves and bring to a boil over low heat, stirring occasionally.

3. Add the spinach, bok choy, and Chinese greens and cook, stirring, for 2–3 minutes, until wilted. Add the cilantro and stir well. Serve immediately.

WHY NOT TRY
You can serve this dish straight from the wok without any sides, but if you prefer to have an accompaniment, it is delicious served with freshly cooked rice.

PER SERVING: 367 CALS | 29.3G FAT | 20.2G SAT FAT | 18.2G CARBS | 8G SUGARS | 6.4G FIBER | 8.6G PROTEIN | 240MG SODIUM

WHOLE BAKED CAULIFLOWER

Low-fat, cholesterol-free, and loaded with vitamin C, cauliflower is baked whole in this recipe and served with a tasty tomato, olive, and caper sauce. Fiber and protein-packed lima beans add to the mix in this warming evening dish.

SERVES: 4
PREP: 20–25 MINS COOK: 1 HOUR

1 tablespoon olive oil
2 onions, finely sliced
4 garlic cloves, chopped
2 tablespoons vegan red wine vinegar
pinch of brown sugar
¾ cup pitted ripe black olives
2 tablespoons capers
3 tablespoons coarsely chopped fresh basil
3⅓ cups canned diced tomatoes
1⅔ cups drained and rinsed, canned lima beans
⅔ cup vegan broth
1 large cauliflower, leaves trimmed
salt and pepper (optional)
2 tablespoons basil sprigs, to garnish

1. Heat the olive oil in a saucepan that is large enough to fit the whole cauliflower in.

2. Add the onions and garlic and sauté over medium heat until soft and translucent. Stir in the vinegar, brown sugar, black olives, capers, and basil and heat through for an additional 2–3 minutes. Pour in the tomatoes, lima beans, and vegan broth. Stir well and bring the sauce to a simmer for 5–6 minutes, stirring occasionally.

3. Sit the cauliflower head upside down on a cutting board and, using a sharp knife, carefully cut the tough stem away. Put the cauliflower into the center of the tomato sauce, pushing it down so half is covered by the sauce. Season with salt and pepper, if using.

4. Reduce the heat to low, cover, and simmer for about 45 minutes, or until the cauliflower is tender. Carefully stir once or twice during cooking to prevent the sauce from catching on the bottom of the pan. Serve immediately, garnished with basil.

HEAT IT UP
To reheat this dish, if you have made it in advance, simply transfer to a roasting dish, drizzle with olive oil, and put into a warm oven until hot.

PER SERVING: 242 CALS | 7.3G FAT | 1G SAT FAT | 34.6G CARBS | 14.2G SUGARS | 9.6G FIBER | 11.5G PROTEIN | 4,400MG SODIUM

CHICKPEA WALNUT PATTIES

These hearty patties are similar to falafel, but have the added richness and flavor of walnuts.

SERVES: 4

PREP: 15 MINS, PLUS CHILLING   COOK: 10 MINS

2 garlic cloves
1 shallot
1¾ cups drained and rinsed canned chickpeas
⅓ cup fresh flat-leaf parsley
1 teaspoon ground coriander
1 teaspoon ground cumin
½ teaspoon salt
⅛ teaspoon cayenne pepper
2 tablespoons olive oil
2 tablespoons all-purpose flour
½ teaspoon baking powder
½ cup roasted, unsalted walnuts, coarsely chopped
2 tablespoons sunflower oil, for frying

1. Put the garlic and shallot into a food processor and pulse to chop. Add the chickpeas, parsley, coriander, cumin, salt, cayenne pepper, olive oil, and flour and pulse to a chunky paste. Add the baking powder and pulse once to incorporate. Add the walnuts and pulse once to incorporate.

2. Shape the chickpea mixture into four equal patties, about 4 inches in diameter. Chill in the refrigerator for at least 30 minutes or overnight.

3. Heat the sunflower oil in a large skillet over medium-high heat. Add the patties and cook for 4–5 minutes on each side, until golden brown. Serve hot.

WHY NOT TRY

Make these delicious patties into the complete burger experience by serving on toasted vegan hamburger buns, with a slice of tomato, crunchy lettuce, and vegan mayonnaise-style sauce or tahini.

PER SERVING: 320 CALS | 24.7G FAT | 2.6G SAT FAT | 18.1G CARBS | 3.5G SUGARS | 5.2G FIBER | 7G PROTEIN | 360MG SODIUM

NUT ROAST

This classic vegan dish is always a winner. Serve it with tasty fresh vegetables and plenty of vegan gravy.

SERVES: 6
PREP: 20 MINS   COOK: 35–40 MINS

1 tablespoon olive oil, for brushing
2 tablespoons olive oil
1 large onion, finely chopped
1 cup ground almonds (almond meal)
²/₃ cup cashew nuts, finely chopped
1¼ cups fresh whole-wheat vegan bread crumbs
½ cup vegan broth
finely grated zest and juice of 1 small lemon
1 tablespoon finely chopped fresh rosemary leaves
salt and pepper (optional)
fresh rosemary sprigs and lemon slices, to garnish (optional)

1. Preheat the oven to 400°F. Brush a small, 3-cup-capacity loaf pan with oil and line with parchment paper.

2. Heat the oil in a large saucepan, add the onion, and sauté over medium heat, stirring, for 3–4 minutes, until soft.

3. Stir in the almonds, cashew nuts, bread crumbs, broth, lemon zest and juice, and rosemary. Season with salt and pepper, if using, and stir well to mix.

4. Press the mixture into the prepared pan, brush with oil, and bake in the preheated oven for 30–35 minutes, until golden brown and firm.

5. Turn out and serve hot, garnished with rosemary sprigs, lemon slices, and pepper, if using.

IN A NUTSHELL
If you're a vegan, nuts should be an especially important part of your healthy diet, because they are a great source of protein and one of the best plant-based sources of healthy fats.

PER SERVING: 289 CALS | 23.4G FAT | 3G SAT FAT | 16G CARBS | 3.4G SUGARS | 3.3G FIBER | 7.7G PROTEIN | 80MG SODIUM

LEAFY GREENS, LEEK, AND ASPARAGUS STIR-FRY

Dark, leafy greens are flavored with ginger, garlic, and chile in this nutrient-packed stir-fry.

SERVES: 6
PREP: 20 MINS COOK: 10 MINS

1 pound 2 ounces mixed leafy greens, such as bok choy, Tuscan or black-leaf kale, Swiss chard, and spinach
8 ounces asparagus
⅓ cup peanut oil
1¼-inch piece fresh ginger, diced
½ fresh green or red chile, seeded and diced
3 large garlic cloves, thinly sliced
6 baby leeks, lower green part included, sliced into rounds
3 tablespoons vegan broth
2 tablespoons soy sauce
½ teaspoon salt
¼ cup fresh cilantro leaves
1 teaspoon sesame seeds
1 tablespoon toasted sesame oil
pepper (optional)

1. Cut away the stems and large central ribs from the greens. Slice the stems into ½-inch pieces. Stack the leaves and slice into ribbons.

2. Snap off the woody ends from the asparagus and discard. Chop the stems into ¾-inch pieces. Keep the tips whole.

3. Heat a large wok over high heat and add the peanut oil. When almost smoking, add the ginger, chile, and garlic. Stir-fry for 30 seconds.

4. Add the leeks, asparagus, and the chopped stems from the greens. Add the broth to moisten and stir-fry for an additional 2 minutes.

5. Add the sliced leaves, soy sauce, salt, and a little pepper, if using, and stir-fry for 3 minutes.

6. Stir in the cilantro, sesame seeds, and sesame oil and stir-fry for 30 seconds. Serve immediately.

WHY NOT TRY
Try serving this stir-fry with boiled rice or vegan noodles.

PER SERVING: 161 CALS | 14.2G FAT | 2.3G SAT FAT | 6.8G CARBS | 2.6G SUGARS | 2.9G FIBER | 3.4G PROTEIN | 440MG SODIUM

PISTACHIO
ICE CREAM

This is a treat you can truly feel good about. Creamy coconut milk and almond milk are sweetened with dates. Earthy pistachio nuts and almond extract give the ice cream an exotic and irresistible flavor.

SERVES: 6
PREP: 10 MINS, PLUS FREEZING   COOK: NONE

2/3 cup shelled unsalted pistachio nuts
1½ cups coconut milk
1½ cups almond milk
9 medjool dates, pitted
1 teaspoon vanilla extract
½ teaspoon almond extract

1. You will need an ice cream maker for this recipe. Put the nuts and about ½ cup of the coconut milk into a food processor and process to a smooth paste.

2. Put the remaining coconut milk, the almond milk, dates, vanilla extract, and almond extract into a blender. Process on high speed for 3–5 minutes, until pureed. Add the pistachio paste and process until well combined.

3. Transfer the mixture to the chilled container of an electric ice cream maker and freeze according to the manufacturer's directions. The ice cream can be served immediately, or you can transfer it to a freezer-proof container and freeze overnight for a more solid consistency.

POWERFUL PISTACHIOS
These little green gems are high in gamma-tocopherol, a type of vitamin E that may play a role in reducing lung cancer risk. Loaded with potassium and vitamin B_6, they can also help keep your nervous system and muscles healthy, boost your mood, and bolster your immune system.

PER SERVING: 195 CALS | 7.5G FAT | 1.8G SAT FAT | 31.6G CARBS | 25.9G SUGARS | 4G FIBER | 3.5G PROTEIN | 40MG SODIUM

Vegan

COCONUT RICE PUDDING

Coconut milk and soy milk make this vegan rice pudding just as creamy and delicious as the traditional kind made with dairy.

SERVES: 4
PREP: 15–20 MINS COOK: 50–55 MINS

5 cardamom pods
½ cup short-grain rice
2½ cups soy milk
1⅔ cups coconut milk
¼ cup sugar
¼ teaspoon saffron
2 tablespoons slivered almonds

1. Crack open the cardamom pods and remove the seeds. Crush the seeds with a mortar and pestle or with a rolling pin. Put the rice, soy milk, coconut milk, sugar, crushed cardamom seeds, and saffron into a large saucepan over low heat. Simmer for 40 minutes, stirring frequently, until the mixture is thick and creamy.

2. Toast the slivered almonds in a dry skillet over high heat for 2–3 minutes, or until lightly golden.

3. Serve the rice pudding hot or cold, topped with the toasted almonds.

WHY NOT TRY
Add some chopped banana, grated apple, or fresh berries to this rice pudding for an extra fruit boost.

PER SERVING: 449 CALS | 26.5G FAT | 19.4G SAT FAT | 46.9G CARBS | 22.3G SUGARS | 2.2G FIBER | 9.5G PROTEIN | 80MG SODIUM

ZESTY
LIME PIE

*This delicious tart features a crisp crust made
with coconut oil and a zesty lime filling.*

SERVES: 8

PREP: 25 MINS, PLUS CHILLING   COOK: 12–15 MINS

CRUST
½ cup coconut oil
2¼ cups whole–wheat flour
½ cup cold water
1 tablespoon whole–wheat flour, for dusting

FILLING
1¼ pounds firm tofu
½ cup lime juice
¾ cup firmly packed brown sugar
1 tablespoon cornstarch
2 teaspoons lime zest

1. Preheat the oven to 400°F.

2. To make the crust, rub the coconut oil into the flour and gradually add the water to bring the dough together. This can be done by hand or using a food processor.

3. Roll out the dough on a work surface lightly dusted with flour and use to line a 10-inch loose–bottom tart pan. Bake in the preheated oven for 12–15 minutes, until golden and crisp. Let cool.

4. Put all the ingredients for the filling except the lime zest into the bowl of a food processor and process for 1–2 minutes, until smooth. Stir in the lime zest.

5. Spoon the tart filling into the pastry shell, smoothing it with a rubber spatula. Chill in the refrigerator for at least 1 hour before serving.

WHY NOT TRY
Try decorating the tart with grated vegan chocolate, a sprinkle of shredded dry coconut, or slices of fresh lime.

PER SERVING: 424 CALS | 19.7G FAT | 11.9G SAT FAT | 52.2G CARBS | 21.6G SUGARS | 5.6G FIBER | 16.1G PROTEIN | TRACE SODIUM

CARROT CAKE

This variation on a familiar favorite cake is sweetened with fruit.
It is also packed with delicious nuts and has a frosting made from cashew nuts.

SERVES: 8
PREP: 20 MINS, PLUS COOLING AND CHILLING
COOK: 40–45 MINS

1 tablespoon vegetable oil, for oiling
8 dates
1 cup golden raisins
1 cup boiling water
¾ cup walnuts
1 cup shredded carrots
2½ cups whole-wheat flour
1 teaspoon ground cinnamon
1 teaspoon baking powder
1 teaspoon baking soda
½ cup apple juice

FROSTING
⅔ cup cashew nuts
3 tablespoons maple syrup
1 teaspoon vanilla extract
1 teaspoon ground cinnamon
zest of 1 lemon

1. Preheat the oven to 350°F. Oil and line a 7-inch round loose-bottom cake pan.

2. Pit and coarsely chop the dates. Put them into a small bowl with the golden raisins and add the boiling water. Set the ingredients aside to soak.

3. Coarsely chop the walnuts and put them into a large mixing bowl with the shredded carrots. Add the flour, cinnamon, baking powder, and baking soda and mix thoroughly.

4. Add the dates and golden raisins with the soaking water and the apple juice. Mix thoroughly. Spoon into the prepared pan and smooth the top with a rubber spatula.

5. Bake the cake in the center of the preheated oven for 40–45 minutes, until cooked through. Let cool in the pan for 10 minutes, then turn out onto a wire rack and let cool completely.

6. To make the frosting, soak the nuts in boiling water for 30 minutes, then drain. Put the nuts, maple syrup, vanilla extract, and cinnamon into a blender and process until smooth. Stir in the lemon zest and chill in the refrigerator for 20 minutes before spreading evenly over the top of the cake.

WHY NOT TRY
Try using orange juice or carrot juice
in place of the apple juice.

PER SERVING: 448 CALS | 16.4G FAT | 2G SAT FAT | 73.3G CARBS | 34.1G SUGARS | 8.5G FIBER | 10.4G PROTEIN | 240MG SODIUM

CLEANSING

WHY CLEANSE YOUR DIET?

Most of us know that health and well-being are strongly linked with what we eat—and with what we don't eat. Many minor—and major—illnesses and everyday health problems can be prevented, improved, or even eliminated by choosing the right diet. For example, two of the major health issues of today, obesity and type-two diabetes, are closely linked with food intake, while heart disease, many types of cancer, arthritis, and dementia are all thought to be at least in part diet-related as well.

Research proves that day-to-day energy, vitality, mood, and brain function can be improved through food choices. Our appearance can also be enhanced by what we eat or choose to avoid. Healthy skin, hair, eyes, gums, and nails are largely dependent on a good diet.

Despite all these fantastic potential benefits for choosing an ideal diet, you may still feel that making the necessary changes will be too hard. This is because, for many years now, the idea of cleansing your diet or detoxing has been used to describe a process of rethinking what we eat and drink in order to cleanse our bodies, in particular, the liver and digestive system.

Some people might consider the idea of cleansing or detoxing as a drastic, short-term change, usually combined with a very low intake of calories. Indeed, the idea of a detox diet can seem extreme and something that you would want to avoid doing for any length of time.

This chapter sets out to show you a different, more gentle, and user-friendly way to cleanse your body and rethink the way you feel about detoxing. This method is better for the body and provides a more healthy diet in order to give it the best possible chance to feel healthy, revitalized, toxin-free, and run at optimum efficiency.

The recipes in this chapter are all easy to follow, and the ingredients are easy to source, being widely available in most supermarkets or health food stores. The results will delight your taste buds and satisfy your appetite, providing an exciting variety of flavors and textures. Most of the recipes are extremely family-friendly, so all of the family can enjoy the benefits of this clean way of eating without having to make separate detox meals for one person.

WHAT IS A CLEANSING DIET?

These cleansing recipes avoid using certain ingredients that are the most probable ones to cause adverse reactions within our bodies and are most closely linked to health and well-being problems. The foods avoided in this chapter are:

WHEAT AND OTHER GLUTEN-CONTAINING GRAINS

While only a small percentage of people have celiac disease, a serious allergy to gluten, the number is growing and people with nonceliac gluten sensitivity (NCGS) have similar symptoms.

Other people show sensitivity to wheat. A diet high in wheat and refined grains has also been linked with obesity and high blood sugar levels.

REFINED SUGAR

Numerous studies across the world have found a link between refined sugar consumption and obesity, diabetes, dental health, and cardiovascular disease.

The World Health Organization recently recommended a drastic reduction in our refined sugar intake.

DAIRY FOODS

Two-thirds of the adult population of the world cannot digest lactose, a component of dairy milk, properly, according to the U.S. National Library of Medicine.

Cow milk consumption has also been linked to acne, some cancers, inflammation, and other health problems.

PROCESSED FOODS

Foods that have gone through an intensive manufacturing process tend to contain E numbers and additives, as well as being high in salt, sugar, fats, and potential toxins.

ALCOHOL

Long-term or high intake of alcohol can cause high blood pressure, heart disease, strokes, liver disease, and digestive problems, as well as depression, insomnia, dementia, and many other health issues.

RED MEAT

Consumption of red meat, such as beef, pork, and lamb, and processed and smoked meats, is linked with an increased risk of some cancers and heart disease, as well as inflammation and damage to the digestive system.

A high animal protein diet may also cause kidney problems.

TOO MUCH SODIUM

A high sodium diet is linked with an increased risk of high blood pressure, as well as with fluid retention, and may make symptoms of several conditions, including asthma and arthritis, worse.

CAFFEINE

Caffeine-rich beverages, such as coffee, tea, and cola, are linked with insomnia, nervousness, panic attacks, irritability, increased heart rate, and stomach upsets and also tend to raise blood sugar levels.

WHAT YOU CAN EAT ON A CLEANSING DIET

These natural recipes will help you to eat a diet that contains all the nutrients you need for health and well-being. You will not be going short on carbohydrates, protein, or fats, and the foods featured are bursting with natural health-giving plant chemicals, vitamins, minerals, and fiber. The recipes are also packed with foods known to boost your immune system, increase "friendly" bacteria in the digestive tract, and assist the liver, which is the main detoxifying organ of the body. Here are some of the important food groups in these recipes:

FRUIT AND VEGETABLES

Fruit and vegetables will form a large part of any cleansing or detox diet. They provide healthy carbohydrates, fiber, plant chemicals, and vitamin C. Many types of fruit and vegetables, such as beets, lemons, the cabbage family, apples, celery, and artichokes, are also known to support liver function and to promote a healthy digestive.

NUTS AND SEEDS

Nuts and seeds are rich in healthy fats and are a great source of nonanimal protein, minerals, and vitamins. They are extremely versatile ingredients and form an important part of a detox diet. They are also useful for snacking on to stave off hunger.

LEGUMES

Legumes, such as lentils and dried beans, are one of the best plant sources of protein. They also contain fiber-rich carbohydrates, plant chemicals for health protection, vitamins, and minerals. They are easily added to stews and casseroles to boost the nutritional value of a meal.

WHOLE GRAINS

If you are avoiding wheat, rye, barley, and oats in your diet, you can still enjoy a wide range of grains and grainlike plants that are known to be suitable for gluten and wheat-sensitive people. In this chapter, we have used some of these tasty health-packed grains, such as quinoa, buckwheat, and cornmeal.

DAIRY ALTERNATIVES

Foodstuffs used for producing dairy substitutes such as almond, hazelnut, coconut, rice, and soy are easily digested. They can be made into milks, yogurts, creams, and butters and provide easy substitutions for dairy products.

OILY FISH

Oily fish is rich in vital omega-3 fats, which offer health protection in many ways. So it is good to include oily fish, such as salmon, herring, mackerel, and sardines, in a detox plan to provide vital fats in your diet.

MAKING GOOD CHOICES

It is important to make good choices when selecting ingredients for your everyday diet. Examples of this are oils and seasonings. For cooking oils, you can choose several types of plant-base oils, but there are a few things to keep in mind.

Remember that many plant oils have a low smoking point, which means that if you use them to cook at high temperatures, their healthy fats can oxidize and become unhealthy. Olive oil—particularly cold-pressed and extra virgin olive oil—has a fairly low smoke point, so cook over low or medium heat for as short a time as possible. Canola oil and coconut oil have a higher smoke point and so are more suitable for cooking at higher temperatures.

For salads, all of the plant, seed, and nut oils can create fantastic dressings, being rich in healthy fats and vitamin E. Try to use cold-pressed or extra virgin oils in salads, because they contain the highest levels of health-protective plant chemicals. Olive, canola, and hazelnut oil are great sources of monounsaturated fats, while flaxseed oil, hempseed oil, walnut oil, and canola oil contain good amounts of omega-3 fats.

To cut down on sodium, there are a lot of alternative seasonings available. Herbs are indispensible. Soft herbs, such as basil, parsley, tarragon, and cilantro, can be used as they are, stirred in or on top of a dish. Other firmer herbs, such as rosemary, bay leaves, and thyme, are ideal in cooked dishes.

Fresh and dried spices can be used to enhance almost any dish, and all herbs and spices are rich in plant chemicals and antioxidants while some, including cinnamon and turmeric, are liver-supporting and form an important part of any detox plan. Don't forget juices, such as lime, lemon, and orange juices, which are great in salad dressings. Many types of vinegar, from sweet balsamic to sherry, apple cider, and rice vinegars, are ideal for dressings and cooked dishes and some are thought to be digestive aids.

You can add sweetness to detox dishes in a variety of ways. Most fruits—dried, fresh, pureed, or chopped—are ideal, and they also add nutrients, fiber, and flavor. Unrefined sugars, such as coconut palm sugar and molasses, offer a high level of sweetness and flavor. Molasses is rich in iron and other minerals. Syrups can also be a good choice for sweetening—from maple syrup to date syrup, as well as agave nectar and brown rice syrup. These syrups also have a minimal impact on blood sugars. Raw honey can be another good choice, because it has antiseptic qualities and, again, adds flavor and sweetening.

Try to buy organic, raw, and unrefined produce whenever you can, if possible, for maximum health benefits.

RAW CARROT, APPLE, AND GOJI BIRCHER MUESLI

Buckwheat grains are soaked overnight for easy digestion and packed with plenty of other healthy ingredients to create a delicious, good-for-you version of Swiss bircher muesli.

SERVES: 4
PREP: 15 MINS, PLUS OVERNIGHT SOAKING   COOK: NONE

3 cups buckwheat flakes
1 carrot, grated
2 red-skinned apples
$2/3$ cup apple juice
$2/3$ cup almond milk
1½ tablespoons dried goji berries
2 tablespoons chopped hazelnuts
2 tablespoons dried chopped apricots
1½ tablespoons shelled pistachio nuts
1 tablespoon sunflower seeds

1. Put the buckwheat flakes and carrot into a large bowl. Core, thinly slice, and chop one of the apples and add to the bowl. Stir the bowl contents well until thoroughly combined. Stir in the apple juice, almond milk, and 1 tablespoon of the goji berries. Cover and let stand overnight in the refrigerator.

2. Stir the hazelnuts into the bowl. Core, thinly slice, and chop the remaining apple.

3. Divide the muesli among serving dishes and sprinkle the apple, remaining goji berries, apricots, pistachio nuts, and sunflower seeds over the muesli. Serve immediately.

MILK ALTERNATIVE
If you prefer a creamier option, you can use all almond milk to soak the flakes instead of using apple juice.

PER SERVING: 260 CALS | 7G FAT | 0.7G SAT FAT | 47G CARBS | 18.3G SUGARS | 7.3G FIBER | 6.7G PROTEIN | TRACE SODIUM

SMASHED AVOCADO
WITH TOASTED HEMP SEEDS

This great combination of avocado and hemp seeds gives you a perfect balance of fats and a wide range of plant chemicals.

SERVES: 2
PREP: 5 MINS COOK: 1–2 MINS

2 tablespoons raw hemp seeds
2 ripe avocados, coarsely chopped
1 tablespoon lemon juice
1½ teaspoons extra virgin olive oil
1 large garlic clove, crushed
½ teaspoon sea salt
½ teaspoon pepper
2 thick slices gluten-free
whole-grain bread, toasted
½ fresh red chile, seeded and finely chopped,
to garnish

1. Put a small, nonstick skillet over medium heat. Add the hemp seeds and toast for 1–2 minutes, then set aside in a small dish.

2. Put the avocado into a large bowl. Add the lemon juice, oil, garlic, salt, pepper, and 1½ tablespoons of the toasted hemp seeds. Stir to combine, then mash to a coarse puree.

3. Serve on the whole-grain toast, sprinkled with the remaining hemp seeds and the chopped chile.

TIME-SAVING TIP
If you want to save a little time at breakfast, you can prepare the avocado mixture the evening before. Just level the surface of the mixture and pour over a thin layer of olive oil to stop the fruit from browning.

PER SERVING: 464 CALS | 32.3G FAT | 4.1G SAT FAT | 38.8G CARBS | 3G SUGARS | 13.6G FIBER | 8.8G PROTEIN | 270MG SODIUM

SPICY BLACK BEAN AND CORN SCRAMBLE WITH TOASTED POLENTA

A Mexican-inspired version of scrambled eggs, served with Italian polenta as toast, this provides a marvelous weekend breakfast or brunch.

SERVES: 2
PREP: 10 MINS, PLUS RESTING COOK: 20 MINS

½ cup fine yellow cornmeal
1 teaspoon low-sodium, gluten-free
vegetable bouillon powder
1 tablespoon nutritional yeast flakes
½ teaspoon sea salt
1 tablespoon extra virgin canola oil,
plus 1 teaspoon for brushing
2½ tablespoons finely chopped red onion
3 tablespoons finely chopped red bell pepper
1 small garlic clove, crushed
3 tablespoons corn kernels, cooked and rinsed
3 tablespoons black beans, cooked and rinsed
1 teaspoon sugar-free chili sauce
4 eggs, beaten

1. Line a 6-inch square shallow dish or baking pan with parchment paper.

2. Make the Italian polenta at least 2 hours before you want to toast it. Put the cornmeal into a small bowl. Bring 1½ cups of water to a boil in a saucepan with the vegetable bouillon powder and when it is rapidly boiling, gradually pour in the cornmeal, stirring all the time. Continue cooking and stirring over high heat for 3 minutes, until it thickens. Turn the heat down, stir in the nutritional yeast and salt, and simmer, stirring frequently, until you have a thick paste.

3. Spoon the cornmeal mixture into the prepared dish or pan. Cover with plastic wrap or aluminum foil and place in the refrigerator for 2 hours, or until firm. Cut into four triangles.

4. Add half of the oil to a small skillet and put over medium heat. Cook the onion and bell pepper for 7 minutes, or until soft. Stir in the garlic, corn, beans, and chili sauce and cook for an additional minute. Set aside and keep warm.

5. Preheat a ridged grill pan or the broiler to medium. Lightly brush the polenta triangles with the 1 teaspoon of oil and grill or broil until turning golden and flecked dark brown. Turn over and cook the other side.

6. In a separate, small skillet, add the remaining oil and put over medium heat. Add the eggs and cook, stirring with a spatula or wooden spoon from time to time, until lightly scrambled. Gently stir the bean mixture into the eggs and serve with the toasted polenta.

PER SERVING: 427 CALS | 19.9G FAT | 4G SAT FAT | 43.2G CARBS | 2.4G SUGARS | 3.9G FIBER | 19G PROTEIN | 1,080MG SODIUM

KALE AND BANANA SMOOTHIE

*This creamy smoothie tastes like an indulgent treat—
however, it is actually good for you!*

SERVES: 1
PREP: 5 MINS COOK: NONE

½ cup coarsely chopped curly green kale
1 cup chilled water
1 teaspoon hemp seeds or hemp seed oil
1 small banana, frozen
1 teaspoon raw cacao powder,
plus ⅛ teaspoon to garnish
¼ vanilla bean, seeds scraped

1. Put the chopped kale into a blender with the measured water and blend until smooth.

2. Add the hemp seeds, banana, cacao, and vanilla seeds, and blend again until smooth and creamy. Serve immediately, with the raw cacao to garnish.

BANANA BLITZ
To freeze bananas, first peel them, then freeze on
a tray for 30 minutes, spaced well apart.
When frozen, transfer to plastic food bags
or containers. Use within 3–4 months.

PER SERVING: 133 CALS | 2.4G FAT | 0.4G SAT FAT | 28.1G CARBS | 13.1G SUGARS | 5.1G FIBER | 4.3G PROTEIN | TRACE SODIUM

CARROT AND CUCUMBER JUICE

If you don't have romaine lettuce, you can use iceberg instead. You can also use Boston, bibb, or other small butterhead lettuce, but you will need two of them.

SERVES: 1
PREP: 5 MINS COOK: NONE

½ romaine lettuce
2 tomatoes
¾-inch piece of fresh ginger
1 scallion
1 celery stalk, halved
1 carrot, halved
¼ cucumber, plus a slice to garnish (optional)
small handful of ice (optional)

1. Feed the lettuce and tomatoes, then ginger, scallion, celery, carrot, and cucumber, through a juicer.

2. Fill a glass halfway with ice, if using, pour in the juice, add the cucumber slice to garnish (if using), and serve immediately.

KNOW YOUR ONIONS
Onions, leeks, and garlic are rich in antiviral and antibacterial nutrients that are thought to cleanse the system. They are most potent when eaten raw, but use just a little, because they have a strong flavor.

PER SERVING: 144 CALS | 1.5G FAT | 0.1G SAT FAT | 30.8G CARBS | 14.6G SUGARS | 3G FIBER | 7.4G PROTEIN | 120MG SODIUM

LEMON CHICKEN
WITH ZUCCHINI SPAGHETTI

*If you've never tried creating your own "spaghetti" from vegetables,
such as zucchini, you'll love how quick and easy it is and how great it tastes.*

SERVES: 4
PREP: 10 MINS COOK: 8 MINS

4 zucchini, 2 green and 2 yellow
2½ tablespoons olive oil
2 large chicken breasts, cut widthwise into 10 slices
1 teaspoon crushed coriander seeds
1 teaspoon crushed cumin seeds
½ teaspoon sea salt
½ teaspoon pepper
juice of 1 lemon
2 tablespoons toasted pine nuts
3 tablespoons fresh cilantro leaves

1. Using a spiralizer, the side of a box grater, or a vegetable peeler, slice the zucchini into spirals or thin ribbons.

2. Add 1½ teaspoons of the oil to a nonstick skillet and put over high heat. Cook the chicken slices for 1–2 minutes, or until lightly flecked with golden brown, turning once or twice. Turn the heat down to medium and add half of the remaining oil, the seeds, salt, pepper, and half of the lemon juice.

3. Cook, stirring occasionally, for 5 minutes, or until the chicken slices are cooked through. Check that the center of the chicken is no longer pink when cut into the center with a sharp knife.

4. Meanwhile, heat the remaining oil in a separate large skillet, add the zucchini spirals ,and sauté for 1–2 minutes, or until just tender and turning golden. Serve the chicken on the zucchini "spaghetti" and sprinkle with the remaining lemon juice, pine nuts, and cilantro leaves.

ZUCCHINI FIBER
Zucchini are a good source of vitamin C and soluble fiber, which may help to relieve irritable bowel symptoms.

PER SERVING: 250 CALS | 14.7G FAT | 2G SAT FAT | 5.3G CARBS | 3G SUGARS | 1.6G FIBER | 24.6G PROTEIN | 360MG SODIUM

BLACK SESAME TOFU

Tofu, made from soybean curd, is a versatile ingredient and works best in flavorful dishes, such as this tasty stir-fry. This makes a wonderful, speedy meal for lunch.

SERVES: 2
PREP: 10 MINS COOK: 15 MINS

1 egg, beaten
1 tablespoon tamari
1½ tablespoons black sesame seeds
9 ounces firm tofu, cut into bite-size chunks
2½ ounces rice noodles
2 tablespoons sesame oil
2 cups small broccoli florets
1 large garlic clove, crushed
1½ teaspoons lemon juice
1 teaspoon crushed red pepper flakes
½ teaspoon pepper
1 teaspoon crushed coriander seeds
1 teaspoon honey
2 scallions, sliced, to garnish
2 tablespoons fresh cilantro leaves, to garnish

1. Combine the beaten egg with half of the tamari in a shallow dish. Put the black sesame seeds into a separate shallow dish. Coat the tofu chunks with the egg mixture and then dip each chunk into the sesame seeds.

2. Cook the noodles according to the package directions. Drain, cover, and set aside.

3. Add half of the sesame oil to a nonstick skillet and put over medium-high heat. Stir-fry the broccoli for 2–3 minutes, then add the garlic, lemon juice, red pepper flakes, pepper, and coriander seeds. Stir for another 1–2 minutes, or until the broccoli is just tender. Stir in the honey, cover the pan, and set aside.

4. Heat the remaining oil in another skillet over medium heat. Add the tofu chunks and sauté them for 3 minutes, turning once or twice. Serve the tofu with the broccoli mixture and noodles and garnish with the sliced scallions and cilantro leaves.

TERRIFIC TOFU
Tofu is cholesterol free and is a good source of protein, iron, calcium, and fiber. It is also quick to cook and ideal in stir-fries, because it readily picks up he flavors you add to the pan.

PER SERVING: 568 CALS | 31G FAT | 4.8G SAT FAT | 49.2G CARBS | 5G SUGARS | 7.9G FIBER | 29.7G PROTEIN | 600MG SODIUM

BAKED SALMON WITH SWEET POTATO AND CUCUMBER RIBBONS

A simple and refreshing lunch that is packed with nutrition,
because it contains vitamins C and E as well as essential omega-3 fatty acids.

SERVES: 4
PREP: 15 MINS COOK: 16 MINS

2 sweet potatoes
1½ tablespoons extra virgin canola oil
½ teaspoon sea salt
½ teaspoon pepper
1 cucumber, trimmed
1 tablespoon white wine vinegar
1 teaspoon mild–flavored honey, such as acacia
4 thick salmon fillets, about 4½ ounces each
2 teaspoons crushed cumin seeds
1 tablespoon chopped fresh dill, to garnish

1. Preheat the oven to 375°F. Slice the sweet potatoes lengthwise into long, thin ribbons, using a vegetable peeler, the side of a box grater, or a spiralizer. Toss the ribbons in a bowl with half of the oil and half of the salt and pepper, then arrange in a baking pan. Place the pan near the top of the preheated oven and cook for 6 minutes. Leave the oven on.

2. Meanwhile, slice the cucumber into long, thin ribbons, using a vegetable peeler, the side of a box grater, or a spiralizer. Place the ribbons in a bowl. Mix together the vinegar and honey in a small bowl, then sprinkle the dressing over the cucumber ribbons and stir gently to combine.

3. Put the salmon fillets in a baking pan, brush with the remaining oil, sprinkle with the crushed cumin seeds and the rest of the salt and pepper, and place the pan in the center of the oven. At the same time, use tongs to turn the sweet potato ribbons over and return them to the oven.

4. Bake for an additional 10 minutes, or until the salmon is cooked through and the potato ribbons are tender and turning golden. If the potatoes need another minute or two, remove the salmon from the oven and let stand while the potatoes finish cooking.

5. Serve the salmon with the potato ribbons and the dressed cucumber ribbons on the side. Garnish with the chopped dill.

PER SERVING: 340 CALS | 18.9G FAT | 1.6G SAT FAT | 26.7G CARBS | 7.7G SUGARS | 3.8G FIBER | 27.4G PROTEIN | 400MG SODIUM

BROILED MACKEREL
WITH CAULIFLOWER COUSCOUS

You won't miss standard grain couscous once you've tried the cauliflower version—it really is gorgeous, tasty, and light. The herbs and spices give a zesty finish that goes well with oily fish.

SERVES: 4

PREP: 15 MINS COOK: 6 MINS

CAULIFLOWER COUSCOUS

1 head of cauliflower

1 tablespoon extra virgin olive oil

zest and juice of 1 lime

1 red chile, seeded and finely chopped

4 scallions, chopped

1 garlic clove, minced

⅓ cup chopped fresh flat-leaf parsley

¼ cup chopped fresh mint leaves

½ teaspoon sea salt

½ teaspoon black pepper

MACKEREL

4 skin-on mackerel fillets, about 4½ ounces each

1 tablespoon extra virgin olive oil

1 teaspoon sweet smoked paprika

1 lime, quartered

1. Line a broiler pan with aluminum foil and preheat the broiler to high.

2. Grate the cauliflower into a large bowl (discarding the core in the center) or cut it into small florets, then pulse in a food processor for a few seconds until you have couscouslike "grains." Add the oil, lime zest and juice, chile, scallions, garlic, herbs, salt, and pepper. Mix thoroughly to combine.

3. Make three cuts across the skin sides of the fish with a sharp knife and rub in the oil and paprika. Broil in the preheated broiler for 5 minutes, skin side up, or until crisp, then turn over with a spatula and cook for an additional minute.

4. Divide the cauliflower couscous among serving plates and top with the mackerel. Serve immediately with the lime wedges.

MIGHTY MACKEREL
Mackerel is high in healthy omega-3 fats, with about 2.6g in a small 3½-ounce serving—researchers often recommend consuming 1–2g of omega-3 fats a day.

PER SERVING: 369 CALS | 24.6G FAT | 5.1G SAT FAT | 11.4G CARBS | 3.7G SUGARS | 3.8G FIBER | 26.6G PROTEIN | 440MG SODIUM

CREOLE CHICKEN WITH PARSNIP RICE

*Creole dishes are full of vegetables and strong on flavor and color,
so they are sure to please around the dinner table. This tasty take on Chicken Creole
is low in calories but packed with nutrients.*

SERVES: 4
PREP: 15 MINS COOK: 30 MINS

2 tablespoons extra virgin canola oil
4 small chicken breasts, each sliced into 3 pieces
1 large onion, sliced
2 celery stalks, finely chopped
1 green bell pepper, seeded and thinly sliced
1 yellow bell pepper, seeded and thinly sliced
2 garlic cloves, crushed
1 teaspoon smoked paprika
1¼ cups canned diced tomatoes
1 teaspoon sea salt
1 teaspoon pepper
2 large parsnips, coarsely chopped
1 tablespoon hemp seeds
¼ cup fresh cilantro leaves, plus a sprig to garnish

1. Heat half of the oil in a large skillet over high heat. Add the sliced chicken pieces and cook for 2 minutes, or until lightly browned. Remove the chicken pieces from the pan with a slotted spatula and transfer to a plate. Set aside.

2. Add the onion, celery, and bell peppers to the skillet with half of the remaining oil. Turn the heat down to medium and cook, stirring frequently, for about 10 minutes, or until the vegetables have softened and are just turning golden.

3. Stir in the garlic and paprika and cook for 30 seconds. Add the diced tomatoes and half of the salt and pepper. Return the chicken to the pan, bring to a simmer, and cook for 10 minutes.

4. Meanwhile, add the parsnips to the bowl of a food processor. Process on high until they resemble rice grains, then stir in the hemp seeds and the remaining salt and pepper.

5. Heat the remaining oil in a skillet over medium heat. Stir in the parsnip rice and sauté for 2 minutes, then stir through the cilantro leaves. Serve the chicken mixture spooned over the parsnip rice and garnished with the cilantro sprig.

PARSNIP POWER
Parsnips are rich in soluble fiber, which can help prevent diabetes and high blood cholesterol.

PER SERVING: 339 CALS | 12.2G FAT | 1.3G SAT FAT | 25G CARBS | 10.1G SUGARS | 6.6G FIBER | 32.2G PROTEIN | 780MG SODIUM

VIETNAMESE VEGETABLE SOUP

This wonderful soup is laden with vegetables and noodles,
making it a flavor-packed and filling choice for dinner.

SERVES: 4
PREP: 10 MINS COOK: 30 MINS

6½ cups gluten-free reduced-sodium
vegetable broth
2 tablespoons tamari
2 garlic cloves, thinly sliced
1-inch piece ginger, peeled and thinly sliced
1 cinnamon stick
1 bay leaf
1 carrot, cut into thin sticks
1 small fennel bulb, thinly sliced
5½ ounces vermicelli rice noodles
1¼ cups sliced white button mushrooms
1 cup bean sprouts
4 scallions, thinly sliced diagonally
3 tablespoons chopped fresh cilantro
fresh basil leaves, chopped red chiles,
lime wedges, and tamari, to serve (optional)

1. Put the broth into a large saucepan with the tamari, garlic, ginger, cinnamon, and bay leaf. Bring to a boil, reduce the heat, cover, and simmer for about 20 minutes.

2. Add the carrot and fennel and simmer for 1 minute. Add the noodles and simmer for an additional 4 minutes.

3. Add the mushrooms, bean sprouts, and scallions and return to a boil.

4. Ladle into warm soup bowls and sprinkle with the cilantro. Remove and discard the bay leaf and cinnamon. Serve immediately with basil leaves, chiles, lime wedges, and tamari, if using.

GREAT BEAN SPROUTS
Bean sprouts are ideal for losing weight,
because they are low in calories and high in fiber.
They are also a good source of vitamin B.

PER SERVING: 205 CALS | 1.6G FAT | 0.8G SAT FAT | 42.3G CARBS | 5.8G SUGARS | 3.7G FIBER | 5.8G PROTEIN | 1,400MG SODIUM

BROILED CAULIFLOWER CUTLETS WITH KALE SLAW

Once you have tried broiled cauliflower "cutlets," you will never want to eat it any other way—they really are delicious, especially served with vitamin-rich kale slaw.

SERVES: 4
PREP: 20 MINS, PLUS STANDING   COOK: 15 MINS

KALE SLAW

2 cups shredded tender kale leaves
2 carrots, shredded
1 small red onion, thinly sliced
2 tablespoons extra virgin canola oil
1 teaspoon Dijon mustard
1½ teaspoons apple cider vinegar
2 teaspoons maple syrup
sea salt and pepper (optional)
1 tablespoon pumpkin seeds
1 tablespoon sunflower seeds

CAULIFLOWER CUTLETS

2 heads of cauliflower
3 tablespoons extra virgin canola oil
juice of ½ lime
1 teaspoon sweet paprika
1 large garlic clove, crushed
½ teaspoon sea salt
½ teaspoon pepper

1. In a serving bowl, combine the kale, carrot, and onion. In a small bowl, thoroughly mix together the oil, mustard, vinegar, maple syrup, and salt and pepper, if using, and stir into the slaw. Cover and set aside to rest for up to 1 hour. Before serving, sprinkle the seeds over the slaw.

2. Preheat the broiler to medium–hot. Meanwhile, remove the leaves from the cauliflower and cut the stem across the bottom so it will sit firmly on your cutting board. Using a sharp knife, cut vertically down about 2 inches through the first cauliflower. Remove the florets that fall and repeat on the other side so you are left with the firm centered piece of the vegetable. Now slice through the cauliflower and stem to produce "cutlets" that are ¾–1 inch thick. You should get two cutlets from each cauliflower.

3. Cover the rack of a large broiler pan with aluminium foil and place the cutlets on top. Combine the oil, lime juice, paprika, garlic, salt, and pepper in a small bowl and brush the cutlets all over with this mixture. Broil the cutlets about 2 inches from the heat source for 8 minutes, or until the cutlets are slightly browned.

4. Turn the cutlets over carefully with a large metal spatula and brush again with any remaining oil mixture and any juices that have collected on the foil. Broil for an additional 6 minutes, or until the cutlets are browned and just tender when pierced with a sharp knife. Serve immediately with the kale slaw.

PER SERVING: 296 CALS | 21.1G FAT | 1.9G SAT FAT | 24.5G CARBS | 10.1G SUGARS | 8.1G FIBER | 8.1G PROTEIN | 400MG SODIUM

MONKFISH AND BABY BROCCOLI COCONUT CURRY

Fish, coconut, and spices were simply made for each other,
as you'll know if you try this quick-and-simple curry for dinner.

SERVES: 4
PREP: 15 MINS COOK: 20 MINS

1 large onion, chopped
2 teaspoons Thai fish sauce
juice of ½ lime
2 red chiles, 1 trimmed and 1 chopped
1 green chile, trimmed
2 teaspoons crushed coriander seeds
2 teaspoons crushed cumin seeds
1-inch piece fresh ginger, chopped
3 garlic cloves, coarsely chopped
½ lemongrass stalk
1½ tablespoons peanut oil
5 curry leaves
1¼ cups coconut milk
12 ounces baby broccoli,
each spear cut in two
1 pound 2 ounces monkfish fillet, cubed

1. Add the onion, fish sauce, lime juice, trimmed chiles, seeds, ginger, garlic, lemongrass, and half of the oil to the bowl of a blender or food processor and process until you have a paste. Put the mixture into a skillet and cook over medium heat for 2 minutes. Stir in the curry leaves and coconut milk and simmer for an additional 10 minutes.

2. Meanwhile, add the remaining oil to another skillet and put over high heat. Stir-fry the broccoli for 2 minutes, or until just tender. Set aside.

3. Add the monkfish cubes to the curry pan and bring back to a simmer. Cook for 2 minutes, then add the broccoli spears to the pan and continue cooking for an additional minute. Serve the curry with the remaining chopped chile sprinkled over the top.

BOUNTIFUL BROCCOLI
Baby broccoli is high in the plant chemical sulforaphane, which is thought to help prevent cancer, as well as being rich in vitamin C, iron, and fiber.

PER SERVING: 346 CALS | 21.5G FAT | 12.8G SAT FAT | 17.3G CARBS | 6.8G SUGARS | 4G FIBER | 22.8G PROTEIN | 80MG SODIUM

ROASTED FENNEL AND ARTICHOKE WITH CARAWAY DRESSING

Here is an aromatic warm salad ideal for keeping hunger at bay—although the dish is low in calories, its high fiber content will keep hunger pangs away for several hours.

SERVES: 4
PREP: 10 MINS COOK: 25 MINS

2 large fennel bulbs
1 large red bell pepper, cut into 12 slices
13–14 artichoke hearts in olive oil, drained, and 2 tablespoons of the oil reserved
½ teaspoon sea salt
½ teaspoon pepper
1 tablespoon white wine vinegar
1½ teaspoons caraway seeds, lightly crushed
1 teaspoon honey
1 teaspoon sweet paprika

1. Trim the fennel bulbs of any leaves and reserve them. Slice the fennel into thick slices widthwise. Preheat the oven to 375°F.

2. Brush the fennel and bell pepper slices with ½ tablespoon of the reserved artichoke oil. Season with a pinch of the sea salt and pepper and roast in the preheated oven for 25 minutes, or until browned (the bell peppers may need to come out before the fennel). Turn over halfway through.

3. Meanwhile, to make a dressing, combine the remaining 1½ tablespoons of artichoke heart oil with the wine vinegar, caraway seeds, honey, half of the paprika, and the remaining salt and pepper. Cut the artichoke hearts in half if they are not already cut.

4. Arrange the fennel and bell pepper slices on serving dishes with the artichokes. Drizzle with the dressing and serve garnished with the reserved fennel leaves and the remaining paprika.

FANTASTIC FENNEL
Fennel contains several valuable plant chemicals, including rutin, quercetin, and kaempferol, that have strong antioxidant effects, as well as the anti-inflammatory anethole.

PER SERVING: 128 CALS | 5.5G FAT | 1.1G SAT FAT | 20.9G CARBS | 8.8G SUGARS | 9.1G FIBER | 3.3G PROTEIN | 640MG SODIUM

POACHED RHUBARB WITH EDIBLE FLOWERS

*There is no need to add sugar to this pretty rhubarb dessert,
because the addition of elderflowers provides its own sweetness.*

SERVES: 4
PREP: 10 MINS COOK: 6 MINS

1 pound 2 ounces tender red rhubarb
juice of 1/2 lemon
1 1/4 tablespoons acacia or other mild honey
flowers from 3 elderflower heads, rinsed, or
1 tablespoon dried elderflowers (available online)
2 tablespoons edible flowers, such as elderflowers,
lavender flowers, and violet flowers
or pink rose petals, to serve

1. Cut the rhubarb stalks into 2 3/4-inch pieces and arrange in a large, lidded skillet in one layer.

2. Combine the lemon juice, honey, 1/2 cup of hot water, and the elderflowers from the three heads in a large heatproof bowl. Pour this mixture over the rhubarb and bring to a simmer over medium-low heat. Put the lid on and simmer for 3 minutes, then turn the rhubarb pieces over and simmer for an additional 2 minutes, or until the rhubarb is just tender when pierced with a sharp knife. Using a slotted spoon, transfer the fruit to serving bowls.

3. Stir the liquid to reduce to a syrupy consistency and pass through a strainer to remove the cooked elderflower petals. Spoon the syrup over the rhubarb and decorate with elder, lavender, or violet flowers or rose petals to serve.

RHUBARB RULES
Rhubarb is low in calories and is a well-known laxative, as well as being a good source of calcium and vitamin C.

PER SERVING: 50 CALS | 0.2G FAT | 0.1G SAT FAT | 12G CARBS | 7.2G SUGARS | 2.5G FIBER | 1.2G PROTEIN | TRACE SODIUM

CACAO AND AVOCADO MOUSSE WITH CINNAMON BERRIES

Here's an unusual dessert that you definitely do not have to feel guilty for enjoying—it is full of healthy ingredients and sweetened with agave nectar instead of sugar.

SERVES: 4

PREP: 20 MINUTES, PLUS CHILLING COOK: NONE

2 ripe avocados, halved and pitted
²/₃ cup cacao powder
¼ cup agave nectar
seeds from ½ vanilla bean
½ teaspoon chili powder
¼ cup coconut milk
⅓ cup hulled wild or small strawberries
⅓ cup fresh raspberries
½ teaspoon ground cinnamon

1. Scoop the avocado flesh into a large bowl and mash lightly with fork. Stir in the cacao powder, agave nectar, vanilla seeds, and chili powder. Blend thoroughly with an immersion blender until the mixture is thick and smooth. Stir in the coconut milk and blend again.

2. Spoon the avocado mixture into ramekins (individual ceramic dishes) or small, stemmed glasses. Cover with plastic wrap and chill for at least 4 hours.

3. Decorate the avocado mousses evenly with the berries and sprinkle the cinnamon over each dish. Serve immediately.

CACAO RICHNESS
Cacao is rich in antioxidants, including flavonoids and catechins—its antioxidant level is higher even than green and black tea, and cacao is also packed with fiber.

PER SERVING: 249 CALS | 15.8G FAT | 5.1G SAT FAT | 32.9G CARBS | 17G SUGARS | 11.7G FIBER | 4.9G PROTEIN | TRACE SODIUM

COCONUT MILK AND STRAWBERRY ICE CREAM

Everyone loves ice cream, but it can be loaded with a ton of processed sugar.
This version is made with just three wholesome ingredients.

SERVES: 6
PREP: 25 MINS FREEZE: 6 HOURS

2 cups hulled and halved strawberries
1 2/3 cups coconut milk
1/3 cup honey
crushed hazelnuts, to serve (optional)

1. Puree the strawberries in a food processor or blender, then press through a fine-mesh strainer set over a mixing bowl to remove the seeds.

2. Add the coconut milk and honey to the strawberry puree and whisk together.

3. Pour the mixture into a large roasting pan to a depth of 3/4 inch, cover the top of the pan with plastic wrap, then freeze for about 2 hours, until just set.

4. Scoop back into the food processor or blender and process again until smooth to break down the ice crystals. Pour into a plastic container or 9 x 5-inch loaf pan lined with nonstick parchment paper. Place the lid on the plastic container or fold the paper over the ice cream in the loaf pan. Return to the freezer for 3–4 hours, or until firm enough to scoop.

5. Serve immediately or let stand in the freezer overnight or until needed. Thaw at room temperature for 15 minutes to soften slightly, then scoop into individual dishes and top with crushed hazelnuts to serve, if using.

STRAWBERRY SUNSHINE
Natural sugars found in strawberries are absorbed more slowly than processed sugars. Strawberries are also an excellent source of vitamin C, manganese, and fiber.

PER SERVING: 198 CALS | 14.4G FAT | 12.6G SAT FAT | 19.3G CARBS | 16.9G SUGARS | 1.5G FIBER | 1.9G PROTEIN | TRACE SODIUM

RAW TAHINI
CARAMEL SQUARES

*Rich in nuts, cacao, and fruit, these truly delicious squares
are great for a healthy dessert or snack.*

MAKES: 16 SQUARES
PREP: 20 MINS, PLUS SOAKING AND CHILLING   COOK: NONE

CRUST
½ cup dried apple pieces
8 pitted medjool dates
⅔ cup almonds
1 teaspoon coconut oil
¼ teaspoon sea salt

CARAMEL
⅔ cup raw cashew nuts
5 pitted medjool dates
¼ cup coconut oil
2 tablespoons light tahini
3 tablespoons maple syrup

CHOCOLATE TOPPING
¼ cup coconut oil
¼ cup maple syrup
2 teaspoons date syrup
¼ cup raw cacao powder
½ teaspoon vanilla bean seeds

1. Line a 6-inch square pan with parchment paper, making sure the paper overhangs the edges by 2 inches.

2. To make the crust, soak the apple pieces in water for 5 minutes, then drain and add to a food processor with the remaining crust ingredients. Pulse until the dates and nuts are finely chopped and the mixture is sticky. Spoon the mixture into the bottom of the prepared pan and press down evenly to cover it. Put into the freezer to chill for at least 15 minutes.

3. To make the caramel, pulse the nuts and dates in a food processor until you have a smooth mixture. Add the oil, tahini, and maple syrup and process again to a smooth paste. If necessary, to make a paste of dropping consistency, add 1–2 tablespoons of water and process again. Smooth the caramel on top of the crust in the pan and return to the freezer for 1 hour.

4. To make the chocolate topping, heat the oil and syrups in a small saucepan over medium–low heat and stir in the cacao powder and vanilla seeds. Keep stirring until you have a glossy sauce. Pour it over the cold caramel and return to the freezer for 1 hour, or until the topping is firm.

5. Remove the mixture from the pan by gripping the overhanging paper. Put onto a cutting board and cut into 16 squares with a sharp knife. Serve or store in an airtight container in the refrigerator for up to seven days.

PER SQUARE: 232 CALS | 14G FAT | 7.1G SAT FAT | 27.7G CARBS | 21.4G SUGARS | 3.3G FIBER | 3.5G PROTEIN | 40MG SODIUM

RAW CHOCOLATE, CHERRY, AND ALMOND FUDGE BITES

These little cherry-filled bites are easy and quick to make—they also contain no added sugar, good-for-you cacao, and make an ideal gift!

MAKES: 35 PIECES
PREP: 10 MINS, PLUS CHILLING COOK: NONE

1/3 cup unsweetened almond butter
1/3 cup coconut oil
2/3 cup raw cacao powder
1/3 cup plus 2 teaspoons honey
1/4 teaspoon sea salt
seeds from 1/2 vanilla bean
1/3 cup dried cherries

1. Blend the almond butter and coconut oil in a food processor for a few seconds to combine. Add the cacao powder and blend again.

2. Stir in the honey, salt, and vanilla seeds and blend again. Stir in the dried cherries. Do not blend again once the cherries have gone in.

3. Line a shallow pan or tray that is about 5 x 4 inches with parchment paper, making sure the paper overhangs the edges by at least 2 inches. Spoon the mixture into the pan and level the surface. Put the pan into the freezer for about an hour, or until firm.

4. Remove the fudge from the pan by gripping the overhanging paper. Put onto a cutting board and, using a sharp knife, cut into five slices lengthwise. Then cut each slice into seven squares. Serve or store in an airtight container in the refrigerator.

CHANGE OF PACE

For a variation, try the same recipe but use cashew butter instead of the almond butter and chopped dried goldenberries instead of the cherries.

PER PIECE: 55 CALS | 3.8G FAT | 1.9G SAT FAT | 5.9G CARBS | 3.9G SUGARS | 1.1G FIBER | 1G PROTEIN | TRACE SODIUM

INDEX